ELIZABETH
· PETERS ·

THE COPENHAGEN CONNECTION

WARNER BOOKS

A Time Warner Company

WARNER BOOKS EDITION

Cover design by Mario Pulice
Cover illustration by Phillip Singer

This Warner Books Edition is published by arrangement with the author.

Warner Books, Inc.
1271 Avenue of the Americas
New York, NY 10020

W A Time Warner Company

Printed in the United States of America

First Warner Books Printing: June, 1994

10 9 8 7 6 5 4 3 2 1

Don't miss any
of the suspense . . .
or any of the fun
of a mystery from
ELIZABETH PETERS

THE COPENHAGEN CONNECTION

Books by Elizabeth Peters

🏵 1 🏵

THE PLANE lifted with a roar of jets, soaring into star-sprinkled blackness. The girl in seat 37-C sucked on the end of her ball-point pen and tried to think of a way to describe the aircraft's motion without using the words "silver" or "bird."

She wrote, "Seducer." Then she thought, "Oh, well, why not?" and added "silver" with a defiant carat.

> Silver Seducer
> Rape

The woman in the next seat, staring unashamedly, started in surprise. The girl didn't look like *that* kind of a girl. She was small and slender, with silvery fair hair that cupped her head in petal-like tendrils. Her hornrimmed glasses were not fitted properly. They kept sliding down to the tip of her nose, and when she returned the pen to her mouth and gazed pensively over the rims of the glasses she looked no more than eighteen.

She was, in fact, twenty-six. The glasses were part of her business costume. She didn't really need them—sometimes they were an actual nuisance. But she hoped they made her look older and more efficient. Her name was Elizabeth Jones. She had been born in Tulsa, Oklahoma, and was currently employed by Frenchton and Monk, Publishers, in their publicity department. This was her first trip abroad. She had been saving up for it for three years. In her desk drawer at home were the manuscripts of seventy-six poems. Six had been published in various obscure journals. Elizabeth had designs on Frenchton and Monk, but was waiting for the right moment. (This hope was, of course, naive and doomed to failure, but it shows what a nice, innocent girl Elizabeth was, even after three years in Manhattan.)

She stared at the three words she had written. It was so hard to find new figures of speech. They had all been used. After a moment she went on.

Rape the virgin sky. . .

No. The sky could not be virgin. Hundreds of flights per week went out of LaGuardia, and it was only one of hundreds of airports. Quivering sky? Palpitant sky? Big blue sky. . .

A gush of unadulterated rapture filled her, starting in her toes and flowing upward to erupt in a broad smile. It *was* a big blue sky, and the plane *was* a silver bird—a phoenix, an eagle, a roc, carrying her to adventure and excitement. She had dreamed of this trip so long; why cultivate a false sophistication when there was nobody around to admire it?

Big silver bird,
Listen to the word,
Carry me away
To a brighter day
Where I'll sing and play.
Hurray, hurray, hurray!

"Now that's really pretty," said her seatmate, in a flat Midwest twang. "Much nicer than all that stuff about—er—"

Elizabeth turned her head, her smile lingering. Her seatmate, mistaking the expression for one of affability, returned it with a flash of gold crowns. "Your first trip, honey?" she inquired.

"Oh, no," Elizabeth said promptly.

"Oh." Deprived of the pleasure of advising a novice, the older woman looked disappointed. "Well, it's a long ride, we may's well get acquainted. I'm Mrs. Hector Rawlings."

"Elizabeth Jones."

"Where you from?"

"New York."

"It's a nice place to visit, but I wouldn't wanna live there. All that crime. Now Jenkinsville, Indiana—that's my hometown—we don't do things like they do in N'Yawk."

She went on to tell Elizabeth how they did things in Jenkinsville, Indiana. Elizabeth's smile felt as if it had been glued into position. The seat-belt sign had gone out by the time Mrs. Rawlings paused for breath, and Elizabeth took ruthless advantage.

"Excuse me. The seat-belt sign is off—I've got to—I want to—"

"It takes some people that way," said Mrs. Hector Rawlings.

Apparently it did. There was a wait.

Elizabeth didn't mind. Her chief aim was to escape Mrs. Rawlings, and once she was out of the sound of that nasal voice her excitement returned. Here she was, on her way at last. If only she could have gotten a window seat. For most of the trip there would be nothing visible outside except darkness, but she could have turned her back on her fellow passengers and reveled in the glorious daydreams that had been three years in the making.

The line moved forward. The man ahead of Elizabeth shot back his sleeve and consulted his watch—one of those elaborate affairs that measures every aspect of life that can be reduced to mathematical terms. Elizabeth smiled to herself. Some people couldn't stop rushing, even when there was nothing to rush toward.

Her eyes wandered on to the person who was now first in line, and her smile turned to a critical frown. Being only seven years away from her own teens, she had for that age group the intolerance characteristic of reformed alcoholics and former smokers toward those still suffering from the vice in question. Why, she wondered, did American teenagers have to look so messy? This girl's face was turned away, but the youthful roundness of her body betrayed her age. The said body was covered, but not entirely concealed, by a garment of Indian gauze printed in hideous shades of lilac, blue, and magenta, with touches of gold. It billowed madly down and out from her shoulders and was gathered in around her plump waist by a raveling piece of rope. The girl's most outstanding characteristic was her hair, an inchoate mass of tangled curls, whose color was ... No. Some peculiarity of the cabin lights must be responsible. Green hair?

One of the lavatory doors opened, emitting a weary-looking woman carrying a fat, red-faced baby whose pursed lips made it look like W. C. Fields preparing to make a scathing comment about babies. The "teenager" made a smart left turn and disappeared into the lavatory.

Elizabeth's knees sagged. She caught the back of the seat next to her for support.

The profile had been visible for only a fleeting instant, but it was unmistakable. The noble Roman nose, the firm lips clamped shut over what had seemed, in certain photographs, a quite impossible number of teeth.... That was no teenager, that was Margaret Rosenberg.

If her native United States had awarded such honors, she would long since have been Dame Margaret. She did have two titles, neither of which she chose to use. Her doctorate was in the field of medieval studies, on which subject she had written several books that managed to combine impeccable scholarship and exquisite style in an almost unprecedented manner. As the widow of a distinguished Scandinavian diplomat, she was properly Countess Rosenberg. Scholar, feminist, and historian, she was also the top-selling novelist on the list of Elizabeth's publishers.

Elizabeth knew these facts and many more, just as she knew every feature of that homely but aristocratic face. Margaret Rosenberg had been her ideal ever since she had read *Tower of Faith*, which contributed to Margaret's winning the Nobel Prize in Literature in 1969. She had used every method short of assassination to get the job with Frenchton and Monk because Margaret Rosenberg was on their list. She had attained the job, but not the meeting she had dreamed of. Margaret never came to New York, and when it was necessary for her publisher to consult with her, Mr. Monk himself made the trip to Connecticut bearing gifts—not boxes of chocolate or flowers, but trinkets from Tiffany. These were not so much offerings to scholarship as an investment in future profits. In addition to her nonfiction writing, Margaret turned out a biennial historical novel that zoomed consistently to the top of the best-seller list, trailing all the longed-for subsidiary rights that gladden a publisher's heart and increase his bank account. Frenchton and Monk waxed fat and decidedly had no kick with Margaret Rosenberg.

"Oh, God, Elizabeth prayed. Let her come out of that one before I go in the other one. I'll think of something to say; something cool and calm and witty and wonderful. . . .

Of course it didn't work out that way. It never does. Elizabeth's only consolation was that by the time her turn came around, she had failed to think of a suitable remark. "Hey, aren't you Margaret Rosenberg?" hardly seemed to meet the standard demanded by such a momentous occasion.

When she emerged, the author was nowhere in sight. Elizabeth did not return to her seat but prowled the aisle, eyes darting from side to side. The bizarre green hair should have stood out like a stoplight—or go-light—but the seat backs were high, and the chubby figure had been short—much shorter than Elizabeth had expected.

She was finally halted in her quest by the juggernaut advance of the drinks cart. She had to retreat, but a last desperate glance located her quarry several rows ahead. Yes, it was—it was Margaret. She looked like nothing on this earth or any other planet, but there was no doubt as to her identity.

When Elizabeth sat down, Mrs. Rawlings wondered audibly what she was doing, wandering up and down like that. Elizabeth heard her only as a buzzing in the background. She was planning her strategy. This was Karma—Kismet—fate. She and Margaret were destined to meet. But perhaps Buddha or God or Allah helped only those who helped themselves. It was up to her to make the most of this heaven-sent opportunity.

As soon as the cart cleared the aisle Elizabeth was up, abandoning Mrs. Rawlings in the middle of a description of her most recent operation. (Gall bladder.) The reconnoiter was carried out with care, for fear of alarming the quarry. Margaret was notoriously shy of publicity; that was why Elizabeth had never been able to meet her.

The author was in the center of the three seats on the left side of the plane. Elizabeth knew why she was not travelling first class; had she herself not written the publicity handout that described Margaret Rosenberg as extravagantly generous with needy friends and worthy causes but reluctant to spend money on her own comfort?

Spectacles riding low on her nose, Margaret was bent forward in absorbed perusal of a copy of *Mad* magazine. There could be no mistake; its format was as defiantly recognizable as was its reader. In the window seat was a young woman wearing glasses, a demure expression, and a drip-dry navy suit. That was all that could be said about the suit or its wearer.

The occupant of the aisle seat was male, blond, and not bad looking, if Elizabeth had been interested in that point, which she was not. It required no great stretch of the imagination to identify him as Margaret's son, whose existence was acknowledged, but not enlarged upon, in her biographical notices. The two profiles were comically alike. The outlines of the noses might have been double images of the same prominent object. Christian Rosenberg's lips were set

tightly, and the quirk of humor that warmed Margaret's face
was conspicuously lacking in his.

Maybe he's afraid of flying, Elizabeth thought patronizingly. He ought to be used to it by now; he and his mother
were always crossing one ocean or another. He was half-
Danish and probably had relatives there, though he had been
raised in America after his father died, twenty years before.
The date was a matter of public record and therefore known
to Elizabeth. Her imagination insisted on viewing Count
Theodore's death as a romantic tragedy, though she had
nothing to base this impression on except his relative youth,
and the fact that Margaret had never remarried.

Elizabeth returned to her seat, Mrs. Rawlings' medical
confidences flowed on unheard as she considered her next
move. She decided to try the obvious one first and departed
again while Mrs. Rawlings was describing her sister's
accouchement. "Thirty hours in labor, honey, can you
believe that fool of a doctor, and then after all she had to
have..."

The big question was whether the young woman in the
window seat belonged to Margaret's party. She could be a
secretary or a companion, or even Christian's wife. However, the latest biographical handout had not mentioned a
daughter-in-law. A fiancée, perhaps? If so, Elizabeth's first
ploy was probably doomed to failure. No harm in trying,
though.

Passing Christian's seat, she swayed and reached out for
support. It was not unreasonable to suppose that a staggering
passerby might miss the back of the seat and rest a dainty
hand on the occupant's shoulder. The fact that the plane was
absolutely steady at that moment would, she hoped, escape
Christian's attention.

He looked up when she touched him. His eyebrows were
several shades darker than his corn-yellow hair. They rushed
together in a formidable frown.

"I'm so sorry," Elizabeth cooed. "I'm not used to the
motion of the plane."

"Sit down, then," Christian said. He returned to his newspaper.

Elizabeth scuttled back to her seat, pursued by cabin attendants bearing trays.

"Say, you sure are nervous," Mrs. Rawlings said disapprovingly. "If you'd sit still, you'd feel a lot better. I was going to tell you about my son having shingles."

Elizabeth was tired of Mrs. Rawlings. "I can't sit still," she said. "I have—er—quiesophobia. A morbid fear of remaining motionless for extended periods. If I can't move around, I start to perspire heavily and talk in a loud monotonous voice."

"Oh, reely? I never heard of that."

"In the final stage my arms and legs go into violent, uncontrollable spasms."

Mrs. Rawlings shrank away, overflowing onto the armrest of the next seat. The occupant, a young man with a bad case of acne, gave her a terrified look.

Elizabeth was unable to carry out her next move for some time, partly because she was pinned in her seat by a tray of miscellaneous inedibles, and partly because Christian Rosenberg's response had intimidated her. She took off her glasses and put them in her purse. Then she opened her compact.

The familiar face was suffused with a becoming glow of excitement. So maybe her nose was a little too big. It was not as big as Christian Rosenberg's. Experimentally she tightened her cheek muscles and produced a dimple. The new shade of eyeshadow made her eyes look green, and their wide, ingenuous expression was an accurate measure of her feelings. Not bad, on the whole; men had never flung themselves at her feet babbling poetry or abandoned their cars in Fifth Avenue traffic to pursue her on foot; but this was the first time a male of any age had looked at her as if she were a piece of rather stale fish.

She finished her meal and half a bottle of white wine, hoping the latter would provide inspiration. It didn't. With

Margaret barricaded in the center seat, there was no easy way of getting at her. Elizabeth had given up on Christian. The only thing she could think of was to lie in wait for her idol and intercept her the next time she went aft—or was it forward?

However, she could not resist one more look. It was a silly, childish thing to do, and Fate (Karma, Kismet) repaid her as it usually repays folly.

So far the flight had been quite smooth. No doubt nervousness on Elizabeth's part contributed to the disaster, but as she approached the row where the Rosenbergs were sitting, the plane did dip slightly. Elizabeth found herself perched on the arm of Christian's chair. His tray had been removed, but he had kept his coffee cup. The contents formed a large damp patch across both knees of his immaculate tweed trousers.

Words were utterly inadequate, but they had to be spoken. "I'm sorry," Elizabeth gasped.

Christian retained his grasp on the now empty cup. He did not succeed so well with his temper. "I told you to sit down," he said, in a muted roar.

Margaret was working a Double-Crostic—in ink, Elizabeth noticed. Pen poised, she looked inquiringly at her son, and then at Elizabeth. Her bushy gray eyebrows rose.

"My dear boy, what a rude thing to say. Even if you two were previously acquainted.... You aren't? No; I see you aren't." She gave Elizabeth a broad smile, bulging with teeth. "Excuse him, my dear. He is a very bossy man. He's always trying to order me around. No, don't apologize. It was an accident, these planes are quite wobbly—small wonder, really—the whole process of flying has always seemed to me to be quite against every law of nature, a great heavy metal box like this, and nothing to hold it up. Cold water, promptly applied, will take care of the problem. Yes. Hmmm. 'A trigonometric function, one half the versed sine of a given angle or arc.' Now that is unfair. Who on earth would know an absurd thing like that?"

She had returned to her puzzle, and was obviously talking to herself. Elizabeth fled. She managed to get back into her seat before Christian appeared, presumably in search of the suggested cold water. Squeezing her eyes shut in flagrantly false simulation of sleep she heard his steps pause and could almost feel the stare he directed at her bowed head. After a long moment he went on. When he returned, he passed her seat without stopping.

Elizabeth was swamped in depths of humiliation possible only to the young. She had indeed succeeded in meeting her idol—and the memory of Margaret's tactful attempt to cover up her awkwardness made her writhe in a manner that caused Mrs. Rawlings considerable alarm. But what a meeting! She would never dare describe the encounter to friends, or mention it at Frenchton and Monk. If Christian ever learned she worked for the firm, he might suggest that she be fired. He appeared to be a petty, mean, vindictive man.

Common decency and self-respect demanded that she leave the Rosenbergs strictly alone from here on. Now, when it was too late, she knew what she should have done. She could simply have introduced herself, mentioning her position with Margaret's publishers; added a graceful sentence of appreciation; and retreated with quiet dignity. Instead she had behaved like a groupie chasing a pop singer.

She didn't dare cry. The eyeshadow had a deplorable tendency to smear. But she knew she wouldn't sleep a wink.

II

She awoke, dry-mouthed and rumpled, to see dawn racing across Europe to meet them. The memory of her hideous faux pas dampened her spirits momentarily, but they refused to stay soggy. So you goofed, she told herself. Forget it. That's Europe down there—old cathedrals, quaint cities, great art, handsome, suave European men—don't let one unfortunate incident spoil a trip you've been planning so long.

She was even able to smile at Mrs. Rawlings. Having forgotten her inspired fabrication of the previous night, she was surprised to find that lady subdued and monosyllabic. Little did she know that Mrs. Rawlings had stayed awake most of the night, watching in terror for the first ominous sign of . . . whatever its name was.

One interesting incident enlivened the hours between waking and landing. After breakfast Margaret passed down the aisle on her way to her ablutions. Elizabeth had intended to hide behind a magazine if this event occurred, but Margaret's slow and deliberate advance gave her the opportunity—her first, really—to observe the total ensemble. The effect was so peculiar she couldn't help staring. The greenish-gray hair looked as if busy fingers had been rumpling it. The blue-magenta-lavender tunic hung limp and wrinkled. Under it Margaret wore navy-blue slacks—conventional enough—but her feet were encased in aged sneakers, originally navy, now streaked lavishly with orange paint.

Meeting Elizabeth's fascinated gaze, Margaret gave her a full dental display and remarked, "Cold water. Nothing like it. Here we are, still up in the air. Amazing!" She passed on, humming.

She was still humming when she returned. Had it not been for the sound, Elizabeth would not have recognized her. She wore a gray wool suit whose tailoring announced "Paris" as blatantly as designer jeans proclaim their origin, and the green hair was concealed under a black-and-white silk scarf, wound into a sleek turban. Elizabeth saw only the back of this creation as it passed superbly by, balancing on neat black pumps and swinging the attaché case into which the suit had presumably been packed. A few minutes later she identified the tune Margaret had been humming. "Long and Winding Road," by Paul McCartney.

III

When they landed at Kastrup Airport, Elizabeth was almost the last one off the plane. She wanted to give the Rosenbergs time to get well ahead of her.

But it was necessary for passengers to wait for their luggage, and the Rosenbergs were among the crowd around the long, undulating belt when Elizabeth arrived. She got behind a large nut-brown gentleman wearing a turban and watched the proceedings.

She couldn't get over the transformation of the grubby teenager into a soigné woman of the world. The weird outfit was not the only thing that had misled her. Margaret was undeniably a trifle overweight, but her plumpness was the exuberant solidity of a girl who has not yet lost all her baby fat, not the sagging flesh of middle age. She could never have been a pretty girl. Those unfortunate teeth, and the nose like something off Mount Rushmore . . . It was not even a classic ugliness, the *belle laide* that attains a distinction superseding mere beauty. She was just plain homely.

But what a face it was! The years had given it humor and wisdom and patience and kindness; these qualities leave their marks just as suspicion and hate leave theirs.

So Elizabeth mused, romantically. As Margaret waited, shifting from one foot to the other, as if the smart black pumps were too tight, her remarkable countenance showed only the same boredom common to the other faces.

The mousy young woman was member of the entourage— probably a secretary. She hovered close by Margaret and was totally ignored by Christian. He was in possession of a baggage cart, whose handle he gripped tightly, as if he suspected it was trying to get away from him. The scowl seemed to be his normal expression. The knees of his trousers were baggy.

Elizabeth grinned, and the nut-brown gentleman, who had been studying her interestedly, beamed back at her. Elizabeth did not notice. She was filled with malicious amusement. Christian Rosenberg was a pompous snob and she was glad

(glad, glad, do you hear?) that he had to arrive in the city of his ancestors with droopy knees.

Gradually a pile of luggage mounted up on the cart Christian commanded, and Elizabeth realized she had not looked for her own suitcase. She had only one. Start out light, her friends had counseled. If you buy too many souvenirs you can always get one of those folding bags.

Her green-and-red-striped canvas suitcase went gliding by—for the third time, had she but known—and she swung it off the belt. For those few moments her attention was not on the Rosenbergs. She did not see what happened, but she heard the result—a scream, a crash, and an outburst of exclamations from the bystanders. When she turned, she saw the girl whom she had identified as Margaret's secretary in a motionless heap on the floor. Margaret crouched down beside her as Christian swung around toward a slightly built man in a worn gray sweater, whose hands were raised in a theatrical gesture of horror.

"You stupid idiot," Christian said.

"It was an accident. I regret—I am injured in my arm, it is weak—"

"So is she injured in the arm," Margaret said. "Get this monstrous object off her, Christian."

Later Elizabeth was to wonder whether her motives were entirely unselfish. At the time she moved without conscious thought, as she would have gone to the aid of any injured creature, human or animal. Abandoning her suitcase, she wriggled between two staring spectators and grasped the handle of the steel-bound trunk that pinned the fallen girl's arm. Its weight sullenly resisted her attempt to lift it.

"It's too heavy," she wheezed, "I don't want to drag it."

"No, don't," Margaret said. After one quick glance at Elizabeth she turned her attention back to the girl, who lay in the sprawled disorder of complete unconsciousness, her face waxen. "What the devil is the matter with you men? Do something!"

In fact, Christian had not been idle. A few sharp words had sent someone running for help, and even as his mother spoke he stepped to Elizabeth's side. His eyes flared with recognition, and she expected a sarcastic comment; but he said only, "Get back. I can manage better by myself."

With one smooth movement, which looked easy to someone who had not felt the weight, he shifted the trunk. The girl's arm was obviously broken. Blood soaked the navy-blue sleeve.

Things moved quickly after that—a doctor, an ambulance, police, and several agitated airport officials. The shabby little man had, not surprisingly, vanished from the scene. His lethal trunk was taken into custody. The injured girl was lifted onto a stretcher and rushed away. Margaret, her trim gray skirt wrinkled and dusty, started to follow.

"Go to the hotel," Christian ordered, barring her path. "You ought to rest."

"She'll want someone with her. A familiar face."

"I'm going. The sooner you stop arguing and do what I tell you, the sooner I can leave."

"Go on."

Christian sprinted off. Margaret stood staring after him—a little, middle-aged woman, her face haggard with shock and worry, all alone and abandoned with a huge pile of luggage. In fact she did not look at all pathetic, but Elizabeth was moved by the image her imagination had created instead of the one she actually saw. Impulsively she touched Margaret's shoulder.

"Can I help?" With some idea of establishing her bona fides, she added quickly, "I work for Frenchton and Monk— assistant publicity director. I knew you right away on the plane; I've admired your work so much . . . but that's not important now. If you would like some help getting to the hotel—I'm not as clumsy as you must think."

Margaret turned to face her. Elizabeth was conscious of a peculiar thrill, like a mild electric shock.

In the past few hours she had met not one but several Margaret Rosenbergs. The face familiar to her from publicity photographs was remote and unsmiling. Now that she had seen Margaret's teeth she understood why she preferred not to display them to her reading public, but the impression left by the photos was one of awe-inspiring dignity and intellectual power. This persona had been supplanted by that of the green-haired girl, then by the sophisticated woman of the world. Now, as Margaret's cool gray eyes met hers, she saw another personality, as ruthless and appraising as that of a judge. The cold, hard look seemed to penetrate her very bones.

The impression passed so quickly that Elizabeth thought she had imagined it. The toothy smile spread across Margaret's face, and she said pleasantly, "You weren't clumsy just now. Assistant publicity director? Your name is Elizabeth, isn't it? What a nice coincidence! You are most kind to offer."

The kindness was unnecessary, as Elizabeth should have anticipated. Margaret had been recognized. They had not gone far before they were joined by a bowing gentleman in uniform, who summoned porters and escorted them around the customs and passport-control areas and into a waiting limousine. The efficiency of this performance was somewhat marred by what could only be described as a continual verbal wringing of hands. "Had you but told us you were coming . . . The Prime Minister will be much distressed. . . . I cannot express my regrets! . . ."

He was still talking when the limousine started off.

As it left the airport and turned onto a highway running through lush green fields, Margaret let out a long sigh.

"How boring officials are. Is this your first trip to Denmark, my dear?"

It was not the question Elizabeth had expected. "Yes, it is," she said. "I've been saving for three whole years, and . . . Why am I babbling like this? You don't want to hear about my plans. I have a business card somewhere. . . ." She reached for her purse.

"Never mind, I know who you are. Joe Arkin's assistant. He's such a retarded old fussbudget, how can you stand working for him?"

As Elizabeth was learning, this speech was typical of Margaret in that it offered a bewildering variety of possible responses, none of them relevant to the matter at hand. She resisted the temptation to agree enthusiastically with Margaret's analysis of Joe Arkin, and exclaimed, "Do you know everyone's name? I mean, there's no reason why you should remember mine."

"I'm very good at names," Margaret said smugly. "I forget other things, though—all the important things, according to Christian. Appointments, and paying bills. But if you want to know the name of the man who invented the zipper, or the woman who is head of the Des Moines chapter of the Daughters of the Golden West . . . I don't suppose you do, though."

"Well . . ."

"Of course you don't. Nobody does. Except the other members of the Des Moines chapter of the Daughters of the Golden West."

"Mrs. Rosenberg—"

"Call me Margaret."

"Thank you."

"After all, we're business associates—thrown together by a strange accident of Fate—"

"Margaret." Elizabeth's voice was louder than she had intended. Margaret blinked at her.

"You sounded just like Christian." she said. Her tone made it plain that this was not a compliment.

"I'm sorry. I mean . . . " Elizabeth had the feeling that she was trying to swim in some viscous sticky substance like honey or molasses. "I don't know why you are in Denmark," she plowed on, "but since you had your secretary with you, I assume you are working on—"

"Yes, poor Marian is my secretary. How clever of you to know that."

"It wasn't hard to figure out. So I thought—obviously she isn't going to be able to work for some time. I'd be glad to help in any way I can. I don't want to push myself on you, but I take shorthand pretty well, and of course I can type."

Margaret looked vexed. "Of course. Women are still expected to, aren't they? Ridiculous. I have always said—"

"I know what you've said." It had become clear that she would have to interrupt if she ever hoped to finish what she wanted to say. "I've read every book, every article you have ever written. The one in *Ms.*, two years ago, was absolutely brilliant."

Margaret smiled broadly. "I like that one too," she said complacently. "You wrote me a fan letter, didn't you?"

"How did . . . " But this time Elizabeth refused to be distracted. "We're almost in the city, so if you could tell me—"

"We *are* in the city. This is Hans Christian Andersen Boulevard. I do like the idea of naming streets after writers instead of boring generals and presidents. Over there—"

"I'm staying at the Scandia Hotel. If you want—"

"You should be peering out the window with all your might. One's first view of a foreign city is a never-to-be-forgotten experience. I'll be happy to tell you all about—"

"Thank you; not just now."

"Oh, very well. Do I understand that you are offering to give up your vacation, for which you have been saving for the interminable period of three years, to act as my secretary in place of Marian?"

"Secretary, companion, whatever you need. I'm sure it would be all right with Frenchton and Monk."

"No doubt," Margaret said drily. "So long as I keep producing best sellers, they will grovel and fawn. I've often wondered what they would say if I demanded a sacrificial virgin once a year. . . . Well, Elizabeth, it is very kind of you. I accept, with thanks."

"Really?" The sudden acquiescence, after what had seemed a deliberate attempt to avoid the subject, caught Elizabeth off guard.

"Yes, really. If you are sure that is what you want."

"I can't think of anything I'd like better!"

"Then you have a poor imagination." But Margaret's smile took any possible sting out of the words. "Now," she added, "perhaps you would like to look out the window."

Elizabeth did so. She was somewhat surprised when the car passed through the central part of the city, where most of the large hotels were located. She knew them all—names, addresses, ratings, prices. Having pored over every travel brochure the Scandinavian Tourist Agency could provide, she had reluctantly decided that it would be foolish to waste money on expensive accommodations. Prices in Denmark were high enough anyway.

Apparently Margaret had come to the same conclusion, for they passed the Royal and the Scandinavia, the Palace and the d'Angleterre, and finally stopped on a quiet street in front of a dignified gray stone building that looked more like the private residence of a cabinet minister or wealthy merchant than a hotel. Roses bloomed in the small garden fronting the street, and each of the high windows was framed in ornamental stonework.

"You had better come right along with me," Margaret said. "We'll call your hotel and tell them you won't need your reservation."

She strode briskly toward the entrance; not until she was almost at the door did Elizabeth notice the small sign that read "Hotel."

The lobby looked like the drawing room of a country house, carpeted with Persian rugs and hung with tapestries and dark oil paintings in heavy gold frames. A mahogany desk near the lift was the only concession to trade. As they entered, a man jumped up from his chair behind the desk and hastened toward them, hands outstretched, rosy face smiling. He addressed Margaret in Danish, and she replied in the same language, taking his hands. Then she glanced over her shoulder and courteously switched languages.

"Miss Jones, may I present Mr. Hage, the owner and manager of this hotel, and an old friend. Roger, this is Elizabeth."

Mr. Hage was absolutely bald. His head and his cheeks shone so brightly that they looked as if they had been vigorously buffed with a soft cloth. He seized Elizabeth's uncertain hand and pressed a respectful kiss upon it.

"I am honored, Elizabeth. But," he went on, with an amused glance at the uniformed chauffeur, who was carrying in the luggage, "what has happened, my dear Margaret, to your desire for privacy and anonymity? Surely that is the driver of the Minister of—"

"An unfortunate accident at the airport," Margaret said crisply. "Unfortunate in several ways." She described the incident. Mr. Hage clucked sympathetically.

"How frightful. You are doubtless shaken; you will wish to rest; all is in readiness."

A charming Old World lift, with gilt bars across the doors and red velvet seats inside, carried them to the third floor. When it stopped Roger produced a key with which he unlocked the door. It opened directly into the foyer of the suite, which consisted of three bedrooms and three baths, a sitting room, a dressing room, a pantry, and the aforesaid foyer, which was filled with potted plants and was large enough to serve as a second sitting room. The last of the luggage was finally brought up, and Roger took his departure, after reiterating his desire to be of service in any possible way.

Margaret kicked off her shoes and removed her turban. Green hair undulated like Medusa's snakes.

"Would you like a beer?" she asked, reaching for one of the bottles that stood on a rosewood table.

"I don't usually—"

"Roger brews it himself. It's one of his hobbies. As is this hotel." With a deft twist of the wrist Margaret used the opener and handed Elizabeth a sweating bottle before repeating the performance for herself. She lifted the bottle to her lips and drank with audible enjoyment, then collapsed into a brocade armchair and put her feet on a hassock.

"Sit down," she suggested, indicating a chair.

Elizabeth perched on the edge of the seat. "Can't I unpack for you? Or set up the typewriter, and—"

"You can sit back and relax. My clothes are all mashed to hell anyhow, and I've no intention of working today." She took a long gurgling drink of beer and wiped her mouth on the back of her hand. "We can't do anything until I hear from Christian. He will telephone after he has spoken with the doctor. Then I'll have to call Sue—Marian's mother." She made a grimace, half regretful, half comically apprehensive. "Sue will have a fit. She's an old friend of mine. I hired the girl as a favor to her, and also to Marian; I thought she needed to get out from under Mummy's wing."

"What a shame."

"Yes, Sue will take a legitimately dim view of my qualifications as a mother substitute. However, I hope and believe that the damage was limited to Marian's arm. Her right arm."

"It would be the right arm," Elizabeth said sympathetically.

"It does make one wonder, doesn't it? About Fate, and Predestination, and the meaning of Life . . . "

Margaret's voice trailed off. Her face was placid, her gaze abstracted; but Elizabeth had the uneasy feeling that those wide gray eyes were reading every thought that passed through her mind.

Finally Margaret gave herself a shake and said briskly, "I will call Billy Monk and make a formal request for your services. I had planned to spend three weeks here, possibly four. If you need extra clothes, or money—"

"Oh, no, I'll be fine."

"We'll see. My business may take less time than I expect. I suppose you'd like to know what I am working on."

"If you want to tell me."

"I'll have to, won't I, if I expect you to help me with the research. I'm going to write about Queen Margaret."

"How fascinating!"

"You're heard of her? I congratulate you on your erudition. She is not well known, except in Scandinavia."

Her voice was grave, but there was a suspicion of a smile at the corners of her wide mouth. Elizabeth abandoned the pretense. "I haven't the faintest idea who she was."

"Good. If you don't know anything about her, you'll have to believe what I tell you." Margaret took another drink of beer before beginning her lecture.

"Margaret, princess of Denmark, was born in 1353. The time was not auspicious. King Edward III of England was ravaging France, the condottieri were ravaging the city states of Italy, and the Black Death was ravaging everybody. Margaret's father, King Valdemar, has been given the epithet 'Atterdag'; some scholars interpret it as meaning 'What times we live in!' You may have heard similar cries of woe in your own lifetime; every generation sees its own troubles as uniquely agonizing. But Valdemar's contemporaries had good reason to complain.

"Margaret's mother—but nobody really cared about her mother. Women were for breeding; they had no other role, except, in the case of royal princesses, to be sold in marriage in exchange for political or territorial gain. Margaret was only ten years old when they married her to King Haakon of Norway. Her son was not born until she was seventeen, so we may hope the marriage was not consummated immediately; it had been observed that premature action in this area often produced sickly stock.

"Not until 1375, when her autocratic father died, did she come into her own. There were no male heirs to the Danish throne. Margaret's son and the son of her elder sister were next in line. The Danish assembly had the right to choose its own king from among the candidates, and they chose Olaf, Margaret's boy. To what extent she influenced the decision no one can know, but in view of her later career, we are justified in suspecting that her role was not negligible.

"Young Olaf was only five. His mother thus became the uncrowned queen of Denmark, ruling for him. Five years later, when her husband died, she took over Norway in her son's name as well. She was twenty-seven years old.

"Like Elizabeth of England, with whom one is tempted to compare her, Margaret ruled by shrewdness and diplomacy, not by waging war. Things were going well for her when quite suddenly Olaf died. Margaret had no legal claim to either throne. We don't know how she did it; but the nobles of both Denmark and Norway proclaimed her 'Dame of our Kingdoms, Master of our House, Mighty Guardian'—an interesting assortment of titles for a woman. A few years later she gathered Sweden into her net, defeating the unpopular king of that country with the aid of his own nobility.

"What she wanted was Scandinavian unity, a dream of many statesmen before and after her. And she attained it, though not as a reigning monarch. Officially the king of the united Kingdoms was her sister's grandson, whom she had adopted after her son died.

"She is the most enigmatic of all medieval rulers. A woman in a world of men, where women were regarded as chattels, she dominated her brawling, ambitious nobles for over thirty-five years, and she was still in active command of the uneasy union when she died of the plague at the age of fifty-nine. She had never remarried. All her energy, all her devotion was dedicated to her vision of union, justice, and peace."

Margaret took a drink. Then she said brightly, "Not a bad ending. I may use it."

Elizabeth would have expressed admiring approval if Margaret had proposed writing a book about the reproductive cycle of a fruit fly. In this case, her appreciation was genuine.

"She sounds absolutely marvelous. I'm surprised no one has written about her before. Or have they?"

"Not recently. And not in English." The telephone rang. Margaret picked it up. "Yes, Christian." She was silent for a time, listening. "I see," she said at last. "Damn. Well, I suppose it could be worse. No, I do not want you to call Sue. I'll call her myself. . . . Will you kindly stop trying to protect me? I can handle Sue better than you can; she'll catch the first plane if you talk to her. . . . Yes, I'm fine. No, I'm not alone. Miss Jones is with me. . . . Miss Jones. The young lady

who... whom you met on the plane. She works for
Frenchton and Monk, by a remarkable coincidence.... " A
longer pause ensued. Margaret's expression did not change,
but Elizabeth could hear an agitated squawking from the
telephone. She felt herself flushing.

Finally Margaret said, "Christian, darling, do shut up.
We'll discuss it when you get here." The telephone was still
squawking when she hung up.

"I don't know what I did wrong," Margaret muttered.
"Maybe I didn't spank him often enough."

"How is Miss—I'm afraid I don't know her name."

"Why should you? Her arm is broken, but the doctor told
Christian it ought to heal without complications. I suppose
the best thing will be to get her on a plane as soon as she can
travel. Now I had better call Sue."

Elizabeth rose. "I'll put away my things. Can I unpack for
you?"

"My dear, you have not been hired as my personal maid.
Get yourself settled first."

Elizabeth took this as it was meant—polite dismissal. As
she left the room Margaret finished her beer and reached for
another bottle.

It did not take Elizabeth long to unpack. She had only
brought a few clothes, and she already hated all of them—
serviceable, drip-dry, mix-and-match garments in navy, red,
and white. When she had stowed them away in the heavy
carved wardrobe that served in lieu of a closet, she went to
the window and discovered that it opened onto a terrace that
ran past all the rooms of the suite. It was an enchanting
place, with luxuriant plants screening the chest-high railing
along the edge. To her left she saw a grouping of wrought-
iron chairs and tables outside the sitting-room windows, but
stayed away from them; the windows were open, and she
could hear the murmur of Margaret's voice, rising and
falling in soothing cadence. Apparently she was talking to
the distraught mother, and finding it heavy going.

Elizabeth pushed through leafy branches to the edge of the terrace and leaned on the railing.

A view composed almost entirely of roofs and chimneys may not sound romantic, but the rooftops of Copenhagen enchant the eye as they inspire the imagination. Red tile and gray slate, gabled and turreted, their pleasant irregularities are further broken by twisting towers and swelling domes, wearing the soft pale-green given to copper by the passage of years. Directly across from the hotel was a steep sloping roof whose red tile surface contained four tiny dormer windows. An iron-railed balcony, lined with scarlet geraniums, enclosed the lower pair of windows. Andersen might have lived in a place like that, Elizabeth thought delightedly. She could almost see him crouched over his desk, scribbling away at "The Valiant Tin Soldier."

Since no one was looking, Elizabeth hugged herself and made low squealing sounds indicative of subdued rapture. Immediately she felt guilty. Her present position had resulted from the anguish suffered by an innocent fellow creature. To rejoice in it was immoral, selfish, and mean. Nonetheless she rejoiced. She had never dared dream of such close, intimate contact with her idol, except in certain of her wilder fantasies—the ones in which she rescued Margaret from a mugger or a rabid dog. "How can I ever thank you, my child? Your courage and quick thinking . . ."

But these had been fantasies, and never, even at the age of sixteen, when everything seems possible, had she mistaken them for anything else. The best she had hoped for was an introduction and a smile or a nod. Now, not only was she part of Margaret's entourage, privileged to follow and assist the workings of that profound intellect; but Margaret was just as nice as she could be. A little flaky—eccentric (Elizabeth made a hasty mental correction)—but wonderfully kind.

There was only one fly in the ointment. Elizabeth squared her shoulders. If Christian Rosenberg wanted to get rid of her, he would have a fight on his hands.

2

THE BATTLE with Christian did not ensue. He even thanked her for coming to their rescue. His manner was not particularly gracious and his smile was barely visible; but that was the sort of man he was, Elizabeth thought charitably. Stiff, suspicious, incapable of warmth. She could tolerate these traits as long as they were not directed at her personally, and she felt sure they were not; Christian didn't even show affection toward his own mother. It was quite in keeping with his character that he should remark, "Quite a coincidence, that you were on the same plane."

"Coincidences happen," Margaret said mildly. "More often in real life than in fiction."

"I have never observed that to be true," said Christian.

"You wouldn't," said his mother.

Margaret finally yielded to Elizabeth's insistence that she be allowed to help unpack. The distinguished author's room was, of course, the largest and most elegant of the bedchambers. It contained a matched pair of superb rosewood armoires, carved and bedecked in Louis Quatorze splendor. Ample as these were, they barely sufficed to hold Margaret's traveling wardrobe. Elizabeth should not have been surprised at its diversity; she had, after all, witnessed the transformation on the plane. But her eyes opened a little wider as each new garment emerged from the suitcases. They included several pairs of designer jeans—the labels had been thoroughly, if inexpertly, obliterated—a gold brocade caftan, a peasant skirt, embroidered and encircled by yards of braid, and an Indian sari of soft turquoise silk. One suitcase was entirely filled with hats, ranging from a tasseled red fez to a purple velvet object vaguely reminiscent of the headdress of a fifteenth-century English nobleman.

She was still unpacking hats when the telephone in the sitting room rang. After a brief conversation, Margaret summoned her to the phone.

"It's Billy, returning my call. He wants to talk to you."

Elizabeth had never had occasion to converse with the head of the firm that employed her, but she had often heard his loud, unctuous voice in the halls. Distance did not diminish its volume; she had to hold the phone away from her ear.

"Fortunate you were there. . . . Take all the time you like . . . Happy to be of service. . . . "

Elizabeth couldn't get a word in. Margaret finally took the telephone from her and shouted, "Fine, Billy, fine, it's all settled. What about salary? You're paying her expenses, of course."

A period of haggling ensued. when Margaret hung up she was smiling smugly. "What a cheapskate. He won't pay your plane fare. But this is not to be charged to your vacation time, and your other expenses will be paid."

"I only had two weeks vacation coming," Elizabeth exclaimed. "And I certainly didn't expect—"

"It's the least he can do. Since you're on an expense account, you can take us to dinner. Someplace very expensive."

After due deliberation, however, she decided that in honor of Elizabeth's first night in Copenhagen they would go to Tivoli. "I know of a wonderful place near Radhuspladsen, where the cheapest entreé is twenty-five dollars. But you must see Tivoli first."

Elizabeth was not inclined to argue. Christian didn't either, but his disapproving frown intensified.

By the time they arrived at the entrance, the lingering summer dusk of the north had fallen, and all the lights of Tivoli were aglow—Chinese lanterns hanging from the trees, long strings of bulbs outlining the facades of the major buildings, rows of antique streetlamps and modern glass globes. Music floated in the air like clouds; they walked from a mist of Strauss waltzes into the oom-pa-pa of a German brass band, and out of that into jazz. Ponds and lakes glimmered with rainbow reflections. The buildings were straight out of a fairy tale: a Moorish castle, a Chinese pagoda painted black and red and gold, a timbered chalet. Flowers lined the path and bloomed in neatly tended gardens; trees and shrubs wearing the young leaves of early summer tied the whole glorious package together like bright green ribbons. Christian, wearing a three-piece business suit and a necktie, was as out of place as an undertaker at a Greek wedding.

Elizabeth was so bedazzled she hardly noticed what she was eating. Margaret had not been joking about letting her pick up the check. Christian tried to protest, but was overruled.

"Be sure you get a receipt, dear," Margaret advised. "Billy wouldn't reimburse his own mother without a receipt."

Afterward, as they strolled along the crowded paths, Christian said resignedly, "I suppose you will insist on riding the carousel."

Elizabeth gave him a startled glance. Then, realizing he had not been talking to her, she gave him another, even more startled glance.

Margaret's costume—the peasant skirt, Russian boots, and a babushka peppered with strident red roses—blended beautifully with the childlike charm of the scene. She looked like a benevolent witch.

"The carousel?" she repeated, in the abstracted tone of one who has been wrapped in profound introspection. "Oh, I don't think we ought, Christian; do you? With poor Marian

in the hospital? It doesn't strike the right note, somehow."
Her fact brightened. "However, it wouldn't do any harm to
look at it."

Having wallowed in travel brochures and guidebooks for
the past three months, Elizabeth knew that Tivoli was essentially an amusement park, and she had had some reservations
about its reputed charm. Patronizingly she had concluded it
would attract the same sort of people who crowded similar
places in the States. The reality had quite disarmed her, but
she was not especially interested in the low-brow amuse-
ments like rides and arcades. In her youth she had been
escorted to a number of amusement parks by doting parents
and grandparents, and had been forced to ride in little cars
that banged into one another, little airplanes that swooped
sickeningly through the air, and little boats that glided
monotonously around a stagnant circle of water. She had not
liked them very much, but instinct had told her that she was
supposed to enthuse, and she had courteously done so.

The first "ride" they came upon consisted of a circle of
miniature Viking ships with dragon prows painted in bright
primary colors. The dragons' teeth, bared in cheerful grins,
reminded Elizabeth of Margaret. The procession sailed slowly around a tiny lake, and the boats were filled with children
and a few escorting adults.

Elizabeth had a sudden, insane desire to ride in one of the
ships. Horrified at her lapse, she laughed condescendingly.

"How sweet."

Christian took Margaret's arm in a firm grasp. "This
would strike just as improper a note as the carousel, Margaret."

"Certainly, certainly," Margaret murmured. As Christian
led her away she looked longingly over her shoulder at the
grinning dragons.

There is no other music like that of a carousel. The lure of
its wheezing rise and fall is an incantation that takes the lis-
tener back to childhood. And this was the most beautiful
carousel Elizabeth had ever seen, set in a green-walled clear-

ing, gleaming with fresh paint and gilt. Snow-white horses with red saddlecloths and golden harness, a giant rooster with crimson comb and wattles, camels and elephants and elfin sleighs painted with flowers were followed by a giraffe at least twelve feet tall, its scarlet saddle empty, as if waiting for a larger and more capable rider than the tots and toddlers who perched on the other animals.

Elizabeth glanced at her employer. The look on Margaret's face, as she followed the musical circling of the giraffe, could only be described as lustful.

"We've seen it," Christian announced unnecessarily. "It's time we returned to the hotel. You need your rest, Margaret."

Margaret allowed herself to be removed from the carousel. But Elizabeth had the feeling that if she had really been determined to ride the giraffe, it would have taken a stronger arm than Christian's to prevent her.

Margaret was not the only one who cast a wistful glance over her shoulder as they left; but Elizabeth was too young to confess this weakness even to herself. She only thought, what a pity that Margaret shouldn't be allowed to indulge herself. Eccentricity is permissible in the elderly, if they are rich enough or distinguished enough.

As they walked toward the entrance Elizabeth was struck by the good manners of the people around them. The place was very crowded, and she heard snatches of at least five different languages in addition to English. She saw only one unfortunate incident. Just as they left the carousel area, a flurry of movement and a series of indignant comments drew her attention to the person who appeared to be the center of the disturbance. He was a very large man wearing a shabby navy-blue jacket and a knitted cap pulled low over his forehead. Since he was easily eight inches taller than anyone around him, his features were plainly visible. They bore an expression of intense distress. Elizabeth had the impression that he was staring at her, which was of course absurd. As soon as she turned her head the large man started backing away, pushing people from his path.

"Drunk," Christian said, as the very large person vanished from sight. "The crowd is getting rough. Margaret, you're dawdling, Please hurry."

"I would like to have a glass of beer," Margaret said.

"When we reach the hotel."

"Here." Margaret indicated an open-air terrace filled with tables. She ducked away from Christian's grasp and trotted up the steps.

"Damn," Christian said.

Elizabeth did not know why she chose that moment to speak up. Christian had annoyed her from the first, and his attitude toward his mother had been a mounting source of aggravation. However, she had determined not to interfere in what appeared to be a private family feud. The crisp, angry comment, and Christian's scowl, snapped her self-control.

"Mr. Rosenberg, why do you treat your mother like a half-witted child? I know it's none of my business, but—"

"It is your business." Christian transferred his scowl to her. "If you are going to work for my mother, you ought to know the truth. She is totally irresponsible. Her secretaries have to be a combination of nursemaid and keeper. She—"

Elizabeth was thoroughly shocked. "Are you trying to tell me she is—I mean, that she isn't—"

"She's crazy. Loony. Weird. Bonkers."

"Yoo-hoo!" Margaret had found a table. She was waving and grinning and beckoning. "Yoo-hoo," she caroled again.

Christian winced. "This is not the time nor the place," he muttered. "We'll talk later. Hurry up before she says . . . that . . . again."

He took her arm and hurried her into the pavilion. Elizabeth couldn't help grinning as a fluting chorus of "yoo-hoos" urged them on. She had never actually heard anyone say "yoo-hoo."

But Christian's brutal, angry speech had disturbed her. Was it possible that Margaret Rosenberg, America's most distinguished literary figure, suffered from severe mental disorder? Was her public image a sham, maintained by the tireless efforts of her son and a series of hired "keepers"?

No. She couldn't believe it. Christian was a pompous ass. What he called "weird" was only a delightful kind of eccentricity.

Margaret had already ordered for them. The beer was one of the famous national brands. Christian stared at his with loathing.

"You know I hate beer. Why do you keep pushing it at me?"

"I don't push it at you when we are in the States. It's only polite to drink it here. The large breweries support many cultural and charitable enterprises. Here's mud in your eye!"

When she lowered her glass a foamy mustache adorned her upper lip. She didn't bother to remove it. Reaching into her capacious purse, she took out a manila folder and handed it to Elizabeth.

"You might look through this material before you go to bed. Familiarize yourself with the subject."

If any other employer had suggested such a thing, Elizabeth would have been indignant. It was hardly reasonable to expect her to start working on her first evening, after a long, tiring trip. And why had not Margaret given her the material earlier, before they left the hotel? Such lack of consideration seemed out of character. But, Elizabeth acknowledged, she was just beginning to plumb the depths of Margaret's character, which appeared to have the dimensions of an underground maze the size of Mammoth Cave.

On top of the sheaf of papers in the folder was a photograph, eight by ten inches in size, depicting a long robe or gown displayed on a headless dressmaker's dummy. The bodice was sleeveless and close-fitting, the skirt was floor length and longer in front than in back, so that it formed a kind of reverse train. The fabric, which was sadly worn and tattered, appeared to be figured in some way.

Elizabeth studied the picture in bewilderment. Given Margaret's penchant for outré costumes, it was not surprising that she should possess a picture of what seemed to be a poorly preserved garment of some long-gone era; but at first she failed to understand why the photograph should form part of the collection of material related to Margaret's latest project.

Then she saw the label under the photo. "Robe of Queen Margaret."

"Hers?" she exclaimed unbelievingly.

"Hers," Margaret agreed.

"But she died in the early fifteenth century. This dress is over five hundred years old!"

"Closer to six hundred," Margaret said. "Her flesh and bones have crumbled into dust, but this fragile stuff has survived. Tattered and tarnished, a shadow of its original splendor, but intact; you could cut a pattern from it, reproduce it—resurrect it as it once was. They called the fabric 'cloth of gold.' A marvelous phrase. . . . It was really gold brocade—leaves, flowers, garlands of gold thread on a deep purply-crimson background. They say this was her wedding gown. But that can't be true; she was only ten years old when she married Haakon of Norway, and this gown was made for a young woman, straight and slim and tall—tall for those times, at least. Five feet five inches tall. She had a twenty-three-inch waist. Can you see her wearing this? Can you imagine her, sweeping into the great hall of Christiansborg Castle, lifting the lavish folds of brocade with her ringed hands?"

For a magic moment Elizabeth did see her—head held high under the weight of the jeweled crown, white hands, blazing with gems, lifting the golden cloth. Her serene, confident face hid a never-ending fear—fear of assassination, of treachery, of ambition. The obsequious faces along her path to the throne were as false as hers. Many of her courtiers hated her, most of them resented her, a woman, holding power over them. Day and night the desperate game went on, a constant series of moves to check and countercheck. And she loved every moment of it. Her firm chin lifted higher, her blue eyes sparkled. She was a player in the greatest of all games, with life and earth as stakes.

A voice shattered Elizabeth's fantasy.

"It is not unique, Miss Jones. Large quantities of linen fabric have survived from ancient Egypt. Almost four thousand years old. Garments found in Scandinavian bogs, preserved by a type of tanning process, date to the Bronze Age. The coat of the Emperor Henry the Second, who reigned in the twelfth century, is in better condition than this, and it is two hundred years older."

Elizabeth bit back a sharp retort. Christian looked so pleased with himself; didn't he realize that his dry little lecture had nothing to do with the magic Margaret's words had spun? But that was Margaret's talent as a historian, the ability to clothe the dead bones of the past in living, breathing flesh.

Christian's smile faded as the two women stared at him in silence. "My facts are correct," he said stiffly. "I have researched them carefully."

"I'm sure they are, darling." Margaret patted his hand. "It was very clever of you."

Christian's mouth closed like a vise, then opened just wide enough to emit a few words. "We must go. Have you finished?"

He led the way toward the entrance, walking with long, angry strides. Margaret did not commit the disloyalty of exchanging a shrug or a smile with Elizabeth behind his back; she trailed him meekly, her expression abstracted.

Elizabeth was conscious of a new and unexpected sympathy for Margaret's son. Perhaps, in his stiff, unimaginative way, he had been trying to enter into her world. It was his misfortune, not his fault, that he had completely missed the point. She wondered if it had always been that way. Had Christian been, all his life, like a small boy pressing his face against the window of the toy shop, never able to reach the wonders within, and never understanding why he failed?

However, Christian was so rude and unresponsive during the taxi ride to the hotel that her sympathy evaporated. I have to stop doing that, she told herself—getting sentimental about people who don't want it or deserve it. There are few individuals who don't have some pathetic qualities; maybe even Genghis Khan had a father who came home drunk and beat him up.

It took the driver some time to maneuver through the teeming traffic of Radhuspladsen and the streets that fed into that central square. They were as crowded with pedestrians and vehicles as they had been during the day. Elizabeth had heard that the night life of Copenhagen didn't end till dawn, and she was prepared to believe it; bars and restaurants, their doors open to the night, blared with music and laughter. The quiet district in which the hotel was situated might have been in another city. The street was virtually deserted, and only lighted windows in some of the buildings showed signs of life.

Christian was paying off the taxi when a man emerged from the shadows of the rose bushes and approached them.

"Mrs. Rosenberg? May I speak to you for a moment, please?"

Elizabeth had lived in Manhattan for three years. She flung herself in front of her employer, arms extended protectively.

"It's quite all right, Elizabeth." Margaret's voice was faintly amused. "I suppose that gentleman is a reporter. He will forgive me if I point out that it is late and that I am rather tired."

"You must forgive me," The man stepped forward. "I would not disturb you at this hour, but I have tried to see you before, and the person at the desk would not let me in. I ask only a moment, madame. I am not a reporter. I am an admirer, and a student of history. I seek employment. I have heard you are in need of a secretary."

Feeling foolish, Elizabeth allowed herself to be pushed gently aside. Margaret peered nearsightedly at the applicant, who stood with his hat in hand and his shoulders a little bowed. His face was concealed by shadows. Despite his humble pose and his conventional business suit, Elizabeth got the impression that he was young and built like an athlete rather than a sedentary scholar. He had spoken fluent English, with a rather stilted accent.

"You seek employment, do you?" Margaret repeated. "You had better come in, then."

Having completed his dealing with the taxi driver, Christian joined the group. "Mrs. Rosenberg doesn't need a secretary," he said brusquely.

"Wait," Margaret said. "I'll speak with Mr.—?"

"Schmidt. Joseph Schmidt."

"But—" Christian began.

"Now, Christian, Mr. Schmidt has waited a long time to see me. Who knows, perhaps he can be useful."

Mr. Schmidt displayed a sensitive spirit. "If I am not wanted—if the position is filled—"

"We'll talk about it." Margaret took him by the arm. "Come along—Mr. Schmidt."

The hotel door was locked. Christian's ring was promptly answered by an attractive older woman whose silver-gray hair was drawn into a sleek chignon. Her smile vanished when she caught sight of Mr. Schmidt. "How many times must I tell you—" she began.

"It's quite all right, Marie," Margaret assured her. "I want to talk to Mr. Schmidt for a few minutes. Perhaps we could use the parlor."

"Certainly, if you wish it."

Margaret continued to hold Mr. Schmidt by the arm, and although he made no attempt to free himself, the oddly assorted pair somehow conveyed the impression of a warder escorting a prisoner. Christian looked as if he wanted to swear. Elizabeth sympathized. This was carrying eccentricity a little too far. She felt threatened and hurt. Had Margaret already decided she was not suitable for the job? She hadn't even had a chance to show what she could do.

The parlor was lit by a number of floor and table lamps, as well as a cut-glass chandelier. Mr. Schmidt blinked, and Elizabeth studied his face, now visible for the first time, with hostile eyes.

He was not was young as she had thought. Fine lines fringed his narrowed eyes and bracketed his mouth. Two handsome plumes of gray hair lifted from his temples. If she had not been prejudiced she would have thought it a striking face, strong-featured, with a flexible mouth and high cheekbones. His clothing was neat but rather shabby. It fit awkwardly, as if it had originally belonged to someone shorter and slighter in build.

"You are too kind, madame," Schmidt said. "Perhaps I should return in the morning. I did not realize it was so late."

Margaret waved the apology aside. "This is my son, Mr. Schmidt. And Miss Jones. Miss Jones, Mr. Schmidt. Schmidt, Jones; such nice simple names."

Mr. Schmidt, whose eyes had passed over Elizabeth with an unflattering lack of interest, looked taken aback at this odd comment.

"Er—yes. Do I understand, Mrs. Rosenberg, that you have found another secretary?"

"Miss Jones is my secretary," Margaret said.

"Ah." Schmidt's eyes returned to Elizabeth. He looked interested now, but not in the way she had expected. A chill ran through her as his gaze met hers. His eyes were a very soft, very dark brown, but there was no warmth in them. They were as impersonal as a calculator.

"Then I have wasted your time." Mr. Schmidt bowed formally. "I humbly beg your pardon."

"I am curious as to how you learned I might need a secretary," Margaret said.

"Oh, that." Schmidt's thin lips parted in a smile. "A friend of mine was at the airport. He observed the unfortunate accident. Again I apologize for disturbing you—"

"Your friend did not see Miss Jones?" Margaret persisted.

"He mentioned a young lady. A very attractive young lady." Mr. Schmidt turned his smile on Elizabeth. His front teeth were noticeably long. The effect was not charmingly chipmunklike; it suggested a more predatory animal, one with fangs. Schmidt went on, "He surmised she might be the fiancée, of Mr. Rosenberg."

"Ha," said Christian. "Of all the damned impertinence!"

"Quite right," Schmidt said. "He was impertinent, and so am I. Good night, madame."

He was halfway to the door when Margaret's voice stopped him.

"Do you read Danish, Mr. Schmidt?"

"Er . . . a little."

"I may be able to use your services, then. No doubt you brought references. If you will leave them, and your address—"

"No, Mrs. Rosenberg. I do not believe we can be of service to one another."

The door closed behind him.

"Well!" Christian exclaimed. "What a peculiar thing, Maragret, are you up to another of your tricks? Do you know that fellow?"

"I never saw him before," Margaret said. "I can't imagine what you are talking about, Christian."

Elizabeth shared Christian's confusion, if not his suspicions. It *had* been a most peculiar interview. She had the feeling that a number of silent exchanges had taken place under the surface.

The door opened and Marie peered in. "He has gone," she reported.

"Fine, fine," Margaret said heartily. "Marie, you haven't met my new secretary, Elizabeth Jones. Marie is Roger's wife, Elizabeth. I'm sure you two are going to be the best of friends. Why don't we all have a little nightcap together? A nice glass of beer, perhaps."

* * *

Elizabeth's dreams should have been exuberant and fanciful. When she finally got into bed, her head was buzzing with beer, fatigue, and excitement, and her brain was filled with dramatic images—Queen Margaret sweeping superbly down the great hall, draped in cloth of gold; Mr. Schmidt, baring vulpine teeth like a mature Dracula; Moorish palaces, medieval buildings, Hans Christian Andersen in the person of Danny Kaye. Instead she dropped into sleep as into a deep well and did not stir, or dream, until a rude hand on her shoulder shook her awake.

She opened bleary eyes to see Christian's face only inches from hers. It wore a look of such malignant fury that she tried to slide down under the covers.

"She's gone!" he shouted. "Disappeared! Get up and help me look. Where the hell has she gone?"

3

S HE WAS indubitably gone. Her bed had not been slept in—or, if it had, Margaret had taken the time to remake it with painstaking artistry. Still groggy, but propelled by Christian's anxiety, Elizabeth made a quick search of the immaculate room. Since she had helped Margaret unpack the day before, she was able to report that certain items of clothing were no longer in the armoire, and that one of the small suitcases was missing. This discovery negated the suggestion she had first made—that Margaret had risen early and gone out for a walk.

Christian paced the room, cursing. The curses were not abstract; most of them were directed at his mother. Elizabeth protested.

"Mr. Rosenberg, why don't you sit down and calm yourself. There must be a simple explanation for her absence. You're so busy swearing you aren't thinking."

To her surprise Christian accepted the reproof meekly. "You're right," he muttered, running his fingers through his hair. "I must remain calm. She does this to me all the time. She does it on purpose!"

His voice had risen again. Elizabeth decided drastic measures were in order. "Sit down!" she shouted.

Christian's eyes opened wide. "All right," he said. He sat down.

His flaxen hair stood up in agitated tufts. He was wearing a robe of singularly violent red-and-green plaid that clashed horribly with his fair skin and blue eyes. Elizabeth found the hideous garment rather touching. Perhaps he had inherited a weakness for garish clothing from his mother, but had succeeded in suppressing it when in the public eye. As she stared at him he flushed faintly and tried to smooth down his agitated hair.

"Sorry. Lost my temper. Must get organized. Er—would you care to get dressed?"

Elizabeth dropped her chin onto her chest and contemplated herself. He had not given her a chance to put on a robe. Her nightgown was nylon—easy to rinse out, quick to dry, and semitransparent. It was a pretty nightgown, pale jade-green trimmed with lacy ruffles; and the curves under the nightgown weren't bad either, in her opinion. But if it bothered Christian . . .

"All right," she said. "I'll get dressed if you will do something about breakfast. I need coffee. My head feels funny."

"Drugged."

"What?" Elizabeth's jaw dropped. Christian nodded impatiently.

"She put something in our beer. Must have. Normally I'm a light sleeper. I'd have heard her blundering around, banging into furniture and dropping things and letting the door slam. She's the clumsiest woman alive."

Elizabeth staggered back to her room. Her head was spinning twice as fast as it had before Christian made his insane accusation—an insane accusation that made a certain amount of sense. She had never been drugged before, so she had no basis for comparison; but her abnormally deep sleep and her present disoriented condition supported Christian's theory.

When she returned to the sitting room, refreshed by cold water and neatly dressed in slacks and shirt, breakfast had been delivered and Christian was pouring coffee. He had also found time to dress.

The coffee cleared the remaining wisps of fog from her brain. Whatever the substance Margaret had slipped into her beer—if any—it had left no unpleasant aftereffects. She was able to contemplate scrambled eggs and sausages, cold cuts and cheese and rye bread, with appreciation.

Christian waited until she had poured a second cup of coffee before resuming the discussion. He looked younger and less forbidding in a pale-blue sweater and open-necked shirt, but his hair was once again immaculate and his expression typically grim.

"She walked right out the front door," he said. "Gave Marie a cheery good morning, and climbed into a taxi."

"I don't suppose Marie overheard her instructions to the driver."

"No. Margaret speaks fluent Danish; she doesn't need an interpreter."

"I still can't see what you are worrying about. She's gone off shopping, or visiting, and will probably be back for lunch." Christian continued to glower, so she added heatedly, "For God's sake, she's a grown woman. She doesn't have to ask your permission to go somewhere."

Christian sneered. "Women have the most comfortable knack of ignoring facts," he said. "Such as the drug in our beer—"

"You aren't sure of that."

"The missing clothes and suitcase—"

"A small canvas carryall and a couple of pairs of jeans! Women often carry a change of clothing."

"Oh, bull." Christian shook his fist under her nose. "Go on rationalizing till you turn blue. The most ominous fact of all is Margaret herself. You don't know her. She's up to something, I tell you, I suspected it from the first, that's why I insisted on coming on this trip. She didn't want me. She tried to talk me out of it. But I saw through her schemes. I've learned to know when she is lying to me. It's a sixth sense, developed from years of horrible experiences."

"You're paranoid," Elizabeth said rudely.

"You don't know her! Her crazier exploits have never hit the headlines. I could tell you things. . . . At first I thought you were in this with her. But she wouldn't have slipped you a Mickey if you were a co-conspirator." He brooded for a moment and then added grudgingly, "Besides, I don't think she would mutilate her own secretary just to make an opening for you. That must have been a genuine accident. Unless . . ."

Their eyes met and, as if by mental telepathy, his new suspicion forced a break in Elizabeth's reassuring web of rationalizations.

"It was something of a coincidence, wasn't it," she said slowly. "If I hadn't happened to be on the plane . . ."

"Margaret would have needed a secretary. Mr. Schmidt?"

"He could have been telling the truth. Margaret has a lot of fans."

"Did he look like a student to you—or a historian?"

"He looked like a werewolf."

"And the way he acted—all those enigmatic remarks. . . . Damn, I should have caught it at the time." Christian got to his feet.

"Where are you going?"

"To find that taxi."

"I'm coming too."

The quest, which in an American city might have proved long and tedious, turned out to be ridiculously simple. Marie had telephoned for a cab, and the company had a record of the call. The only stumbling block was Christian's ineptitude with the language, which Elizabeth persisted in thinking of as his native tongue. She listened critically as he attempted to interrogate the driver in stumbling Danish. Finally he got the point across. The driver agreed to take them to the place where he had taken the lady. They piled into the cab.

"You don't speak the language very well," Elizabeth remarked.

"I don't have occasion to use it."

"Your native language—"

"My native language is English. I'm an American citizen."

"You needn't sound so aggressive."

"I am not aggressive. I have nothing against Denmark or the Danish language. Nor do I have any sentimental attachment to them."

"You should be proud of your heritage. This beautiful, picturesque city—"

"The picturesque does not attract me. I prefer Manhattan."

"Dirty, ugly, crime-ridden—"

"Modern, up-to-date, looking to the future instead of clinging to the past."

Elizabeth abandoned the argument. The man had no more romance in his soul than a codfish.

The cab came to a halt in front of an imposing building formed of the soft pinky-rose bricks that give Copenhagen so much of its charm.

"I'll be damned," Christian said, staring out the window. "It's a museum. I think I remember this place. Carlsberg something."

"*Ja, ja.*" The driver nodded enthusiastically. "Glyptothek Ny Carlsberg—museum, very good, very interesting. Ten kroner, please."

Christian obliged. "It is one of Margaret's favorite museums," he said, "Maybe she did decide to go sightseeing . . . damn her."

"I know about this place," Elizabeth said, as they mounted the stairs. "Post-impressionist painting and classical antiquities. Which does Margaret prefer?"

"The antiquities, I would guess. Though, with Margaret, you never know."

Egyptian, Greek, Roman, Etruscan; stately statues and fluted columns; the exhibits were interesting enough, if one were interested, to entertain a visitor for hours. However, a rapid tour of the halls showed no sign of Margaret. Returning to the central court, a charming arrangement of palms and other exotic plants surrounding a tinkling fountain, Christian dropped onto a marble bench and surpassed his earlier attempts at profanity.

"She's come and gone. But why the devil would she come here in the first place?"

Elizabeth was beginning to share his exasperation. "I can't imagine. Does she know the director, by any chance?"

"Probably. She knows everybody. Ministers of state, bums, concert violinists, pickpockets. . . . Let's ask the guards if they remember seeing her."

One of the guards knew enough English to nod at Christian's description. The lady in the black dress, the lady with the large nose and many teeth, had indeed entered the museum. No, she had not asked for the director. She had not spoken at all, she had only displayed the teeth. She had not gone out. At any rate, he had not seen her go.

"Let's have another look around," Elizabeth suggested. "Maybe we missed her. She could have gone to the ladies' room—"

"Oh, God," Christian shouted. "God damn it to hell! I should have thought of it. Get in there, Elizabeth. Don't bother looking for Margaret. Look for her clothes."

They weren't hard to find. Neatly rolled and pushed into the metal bin devoted to used paper towels was a black suit, a black-and-white scarf, and a pair of black pumps.

A second interrogation of the guards produced shrugs and indignation. How could they be expected to remember a small plump woman wearing blue jeans? The museum was popular with students, and nine-tenths of the students, male and female, Danish and foreign, chubby and slim, wore blue jeans. To distinguish one from the countless others was impossible.

Elizabeth led a frenzied Christian from the museum. "Where to now?" she asked.

"Back to the hotel. Maybe she's turned up."

She had not turned up. However, she had telephoned.

"There, you see," Elizabeth said. "I told you you were making a fuss about nothing."

Christian ignored her. "What was the message?" he demanded of Marie, who was on duty at the desk.

She smiled. "You are to take Miss Jones sightseeing."

"Great," Elizabeth said. The whirlwind tour of the museum had whetted her appetite. That was what she had come for, after all—sightseeing. "I want to see the Little Mermaid," she added.

Christian continued to behave as if she did not exist. "What was the message?" he repeated.

"Ho, ho," said Marie. She winked at Elizabeth. "These young men, they are all the same; they think Mama or Papa is not sensible. Always they wish to supervise. For the middle-aged as for the young, independence is necessary, is it not?"

"Absolutely," Elizabeth said.

"But you wish to hear the message?" She smiled at Christian, who nodded speechlessly. In a leisurely fashion Marie searched through a pile of slips on the desk. "Here it is. 'Unavoidably detained. Take Elizabeth sightseeing.' As I told you."

"That was all?" Christian demanded.

"What more should there be?"

Christian refused to see the Little Mermaid. He had a number of rude things to say about the Little Mermaid. He used words like "sentimental," "tasteless," and "touristy." He didn't even want to leave the hotel to eat lunch, but after she had watched him pace the length of the sitting room a hundred and ten times, Elizabeth insisted they go out. She knew that if she saw him walk the same strip of carpet one more time she would hit him with something.

In the lobby she paused for a moment to make sure her guidebook was in her purse. Perhaps food would soften his mood, and she could persuade him to follow Margaret's suggestion. At the moment the mood was far from promising. Christian didn't even wait for her, but stormed out of the hotel so furiously that he almost ran into a beggar who had taken up a position outside the hotel. The unfortunate man jumped back just in time, clapping one hand to his face as if to hold in place the dark glasses that explained his disability.

Elizabeth stopped and added a handful of coins to the pitiful collection in his cap. She had to run to catch up with Christian.

As they walked toward the city center, increasing pedestrian traffic forced him to slow his pace. Elizabeth was enjoying the walk. The weather was beautifully sunny and cool, and there were sights aplenty to see—handsome old houses, pretty gardens, and ancient church or two. Eventually they turned into a broad street closed to vehicular traffic and filled from side to side with pedestrians. Elizabeth tugged at Christian's sleeve.

"Stroget?" she asked.

"What are you talking about?"

"Is this Stroget? The pedestrians-only shopping street? I read about it in my guidebook."

"The street sign said 'Ostergade.' "

"It isn't *named* Stroget; people *call* it that. Don't you know anything about Copenhagen?"

"I know all I want to know." He added, with a disgusted survey of the scene, "Is this your idea of picturesque? Unkempt youths sprawled on the sidewalk, Wimpy's and soft ice cream stands, loudmouthed tourists making fools of themselves. . . . It reminds me of some parts of Sixth Avenue, only these people are wearing weirder clothes."

Elizabeth sighed. "Where are we going to eat?"

"I don't know and I don't care."

"I'm hungry."

"Humph." Christian stopped and stared vaguely around, as if trying to orient himself. They found themselves on the fringes of a group of people who had gathered to listen to a young man strumming a guitar and singing in a high-pitched nasal voice.

"Summertime sickness, pains in the gut," he howled.

A guitar case, open on the ground in front of him, invited contributions. Elizabeth reached in her purse.

"You aren't going to give money to that degenerate, are you?" Christian demanded in outraged tones.

"He sounds like an American," Elizabeth murmured. "A wandering student, singing his way across Europe."

"Anybody who sings like that deserves to starve to death."

The singer's voice rose to a shriek. "Puking all over the streets of the world," he cried.

Elizabeth allowed herself to be drawn away.

There were other performers, some playing accordions, some mouth organs. Guitars were the most popular instrument, but they saw one combo consisting solely of percussion instruments, which made an unholy din but did at least drown out the voices of the singers. Christian finally settled on an open-air café, in a small square, midway between two musical ensembles, where the conflicting beats more or less canceled one another out. He ordered without giving Elizabeth a chance to consult the menu.

"You spoke Danish," she said, too surprised to object to his high-handed manner.

"Did I?" Turned half away from her, his eyes scanned the faces of passersby.

"Will you stop that? The chance of her passing this place at this particular moment are about a million to one."

"We aren't far from the university. She likes sections of that sort; weird, far-out, crazy people. She'd have given money to that howling maniac."

"Christian . . . " It was the first time she had addressed him by his given name; again, as she had done the previous night at Tivoli, she sensed the hurt and worry concealed by his manner.

"I'm going about this the wrong way," Christian muttered. He turned his chair around to face hers. "I've been yelling and cursing and losing my temper. I can't blame you for thinking I am acting unreasonably. May I explain to you why I am concerned?"

"Certainly."

"I'll have to give you some background first."

"I've got all day."

"It may take all day. You know what I do for a living, don't you? You must; those damned publicity releases mention me. I'm a broker. A dull, money-grubbing, materialistic manipulator of other people's money. I like it. I'm good at it, too—or I would be, if I didn't have to spend so much time managing Margaret. You think I bully her, don't you? You think I enjoy it? Hell, I have a life of my own to lead! If I had my way, I wouldn't go near her or her damned money. But if I didn't handle it she'd be broke and bankrupt. Sure, she makes a bundle. She also spends it as fast as it comes in. Handouts to every loser who comes whining to her with a pathetic story, contributions to causes like 'Save the Oysters,' impulse buying on a level you can't begin to imagine. Do you know what she wanted to buy last year? A carousel."

"A what? You mean a music box in the shape of—"

"A carousel! A whole, real, full-sized, antique merry-go-round. She's crazy about them."

"Well! That is rather . . . But antiques are a good investment. I've seen carousel horses in museums."

"So have I. I know more about investments, including American antiques, than you do. She wasn't interested in its potential value. She wanted to set it up in the barn—she bought the barn three years ago and had it moved to her property—so she could ride on it whenever she was in the mood."

"I see."

"I'm telling you this, which is none of your business—and if I ever see any of it in your publicity releases, I'll sue—because you have to understand what sort of woman Margaret is. Oh, she's brilliant, I don't deny that. When she sits down at her desk with pen in hand, she is a master of her craft. Nobody does it better. When she is anywhere else she is a demented child with an imagination wilder than any drug addict's."

"Come on, now. You're exaggerating."

"I have to watch over her. She needs me."

"I'm sure she does," Elizabeth said gently.

"All right. With that in mind, let me tell you what led up to this trip. Once you've heard the facts you'll agree that something is rotten in the state of . . . I didn't intend to say that."

"It's very good," Elizabeth said encouragingly.

"Humph.

The waiter brought their food. Elizabeth had been hoping for some exotic delicacy, smothered in wine sauce or sour cream. What she got was steak and potatoes. Just like a man, she thought disgustedly.

Christian went on with his lecture. "Two weeks ago I went to visit her. She was hard at work on her new novel. It's about Boudicca—if that's how you pronounce it—the ancient British queen who fought the Romans. Margaret had finished about a hundred fifty pages and was going strong. I don't know whether you are familiar with her working methods; she has a hard time starting each book, but once she gets rolling she stays at it night and day. She wasn't keen on my coming when I did, but I had some business matters that wouldn't wait.

"We spent the evening in the library. I was reading the manuscript while Margaret opened her mail—she always waits till after dinner to read it, says it distracts her if she stops work in the middle of the day. Anyhow, I was absorbed in the story—it is going to be one of her best—but before long I came across a passage I thought needed amplification. I looked up.

"Margaret was sitting bolt upright in her chair staring at a letter. I've never seen such a look on her face. It was . . . I can't describe it."

"Deadly white?" Elizabeth suggested. "Rigid with horror? A ghastly mask of consternation? No, that isn't—"

"No, it isn't. She was rigid, all right, but not with horror. Surprise, maybe. Incredulity. Astonished disbelief mingled with anticipation. The face of someone who has seen her most incredible dream—"

"I get the point."

"So I said, 'What's the matter?' And she said, 'Nothing, darling, such a funny fan letter.' And I said, 'Let me read it, you know I enjoy your weird mail,' and she said . . . I forget what she said, it was one of those loony nonsequiturs of hers. She bolted out of the room. when I followed I found she had locked herself in the john. She wouldn't come out, even when I banged on the door."

Elizabeth was unable to repress a smile. "That was not the smartest thing in the world to do."

"Maybe not. I lose my smarts around Margaret. She has a very peculiar effect on my brain. Anyhow, I decided not to pursue the matter. A week later, after I had returned to New York, I got a call from a friend of mine who works in the local travel agency, telling me Margaret had ordered a ticket to Copenhagen."

"A friend? Don't you mean a spy? Really, Christian, if you sink to such depths it's no wonder your mother tries to get away from you."

"I don't like to do it. I have to." Christian took a bite of his cooling food. "Anyway," he resumed, before Elizabeth could answer, "when I accused her, she admitted the truth. She said her book had gone stale, and she had a new idea she wanted to work on. The Margaret biography."

"Books do go stale."

"Not hers. Besides—you haven't had time to do any reading about this medieval queen, have you? Believe me, there is not enough material available for the kind of book Margaret writes—in-depth studies of personality and behavior."

"It could be a generalized medieval history, using Queen Margaret as a focal point. That sort of thing has been done, quite successfully."

"Maybe. That's a minor point. But when you add it to the other peculiar incidents . . . I insisted on coming with her, of course. She argued for a while, and then gave in.

"Now think over what has happened since we arrived yesterday. The accident at the airport could have been a genuine accident; but doesn't it strike you as somewhat suspicious that Margaret's secretary was the one immobilized, and that some character should turn up to apply for the job only a few hours later? Now Margaret is gone, without a word of explanation."

"The telephone call—"

"I don't believe she was the one who called."

Elizabeth put her fork down, feeling the food she had eaten weigh heavily at the base of her stomach. "Are you suggesting that she has been kidnapped?"

"She's a wealthy woman. Thanks to me."

"She walked out of the hotel on her own two feet."

"She may have been snatched on the street. Or lured to a lonely spot. Margaret can be lured almost anywhere, with the right kind of appeal."

"Kidnappers send ransom notes."

"Sooner or later they do," Christian agreed. He glanced at his watch. "It's after four o'clock. I'm going to call the hotel. If she hasn't turned up I am going to the police. Do you want to come with me, or would you rather sit here and stuff yourself on dessert?"

He indicated a heavily laden pastry cart which a waitress was pushing in their direction. Fresh red strawberries and yellow cream, meringues, tarts loaded with fruit.

Elizabeth swallowed. "Not very likely," she said bitterly.

II

Police headquarters was located, logically enough, on Polititorvet. According to Christian, one of the top officials was an old friend of Margaret's. They could cut through a tangle of red tape by going directly to him.

The building was a somber gray stucco block, featureless and forbidding—one of the few unattractive buildings in the city. The name of chief Inspector Grundtvig won an immediate and respectful reaction from the young policeman at the information desk. A uniformed escort led them up stairs and along corridors to a large office overlooking the harbor. Actually, Elizabeth was never really sure what Grundtvig's title was; the Danish equivalent sounded like a gargle and a grunt, and nobody bothered to translate it for her. But he looked like a chief inspector, or perhaps a jolly, jovial burgomaster in a German folk tale. His hair was snow white and so thick and shiny that it resembled an extremely expensive wig. His cheeks were round and pink, his chins extensive. Eyes of clear brilliant blue beamed from under bushy white eyebrows. They had barely entered the room before he came bounding to meet them. He wrung Christian's hand with genial ferocity.

"I would know you anywhere, my young friend! You are the image of your distinguished father! You don't remember old Grundtvig, I suppose—no, why the devil should you, you were only so high the last time I saw you." He measured an improbable height, scant inches off the floor, with one big hand. "But forgive me," he went on, turning his benevolent smile on Elizabeth. "In my pleasure to see you I am rude, and to such a beautiful young lady! Your fiancée, I suppose? You are a lucky fellow. What is your name, my dear lady?"

"Her name is Elizabeth Jones, and she is not my fiancée," Christian said.

"No? What a pity for you. Please sit down, Miss Jones, Christian—I may call you that, I hope, since we are old friends. And how is my dear Margaret? I look forward to seeing her so much; but I know she is always busy when she comes. So many friends, so many things to do."

"You don't seem surprised to see me," Christian said. "Did Margaret tell you she was coming?"

"Aha!" Grundtvig waved a plump finger at him. "You should never ask how a policeman gets his information."

"Oh," Christian nodded. "The accident at the airport, of course."

"Precisely. Normally such a minor matter would not come to my attention, but the name of your distinguished mother . . . It was the first I had heard of her coming, so I assumed she wished to be private. I therefore made sure the matter was not reported in the press." Grundtvig shuffled through a stack of papers. "Yes, here is the report. You have come at Margaret's request, to inquire what progress we have made? Most unsatisfactory. I am ashamed. The criminal has vanished without a trace." He shook his head sadly.

Christian was silent, thrown off the track by the rapid flow of information he had not expected nor requested. Elizabeth said hesitantly, "Excuse me, but why do you call him a criminal? It was an accident."

"The man was obviously mad," Grundtvig said seriously. "We opened his trunk, you see. It contained nothing but a lot of heavy stones wrapped in rags. He may be a member of some terrorist organization, hurling trunks at people in random rage. We would like very much to apprehend him. The descriptions of eyewitnesses were vague and conflicting, as they usually are. You have perhaps a better description?"

"There was nothing distinctive about him," Christian said. "He was a nondescript little man, with ordinary features."

"A pity. You will tell my dear Margaret that we will continue to search for him."

Christian hesitated. Elizabeth hoped he had thought better of his intention of reporting his mother missing, but she had underestimated his stubbornness.

"I would tell her if I could. As a matter of fact, that's why I came; it wasn't about the accident. Margaret has disappeared."

Grundtvig leaned back in his chair and folded his hands over his round little stomach. "Disappeared? A strange word to use, my young friend. Tell me about it."

Elizabeth had to admit that Christian made a poor job of the telling. Grundtvig's faint smile and steady stare didn't make the task any easier. When Christian had stuttered to a stop, the police officer's smile broadened.

"So she has been missing since eight this morning. Nine hours."

"It isn't the length of time, it's the circumstances," Christian insisted. "The accident, the man who called himself Schmidt—"

"Yes, yes, very interesting. You have your mother's talent for fiction, young Christian. No"—for Christian, now flushed and angry, would have interrupted—"no, forgive my rudeness. I should not make light of your feelings. But don't you see that each of these facts has an innocent explanation? You know your mother as well as I. This is not the first time she has wandered off on some project of her own."

"It isn't?" Elizabeth exclaimed.

Grundtvig chuckled fatly. "We, her friends, try to keep her little tricks out of the newspapers, my dear. But yes, Margaret is given to running away. The last time, if I recall, she wished to learn how to jump with a parachute. How long was she 'missing' that time, young Christian?"

"A week." The sound of Christian's teeth gritting was distinctly audible. He added furiously, "The course took two weeks, but she broke her leg."

Grundtvig grinned. "She forgot to bend her knees and roll. Always you must roll when—"

"How did you find out about that?" Christian demanded. "It happened three years ago, in upper New York. I thought I had succeeded in keeping it quiet."

"Oh, she wrote me about it. She thought it very amusing. The time before that, she went with the rock-music group, do you remember? What was its name? Pinky Green, or Greenish Purple—"

"I have done my best to forget the name, and the incident." Christian clutched his brow. "You think it's funny. I don't. Do you know about the time before *that?* The meeting with Obi Franken?"

"The Black Panther, yes. So many colors," Grundtvig said musingly. "Pinks and greens and blacks . . . It must be a weakness of Margaret's." Seeing that Christian was on the verge of exploding, he added hastily, "No young Christian, I have not forgotten that, nor should you. The man was a fugitive; ten years or more he had eluded the law. He asked her to come to him, she was the only person he would speak to. For two days they sat in his cabin in New England, drinking beer and discussing Aristotle. Then he turned himself in. She did a good service then, to Mr. Obi and to her country. How do you know she is not on another such mission now, a mission where secrecy is vital?"

"That's what worries me." Christian continued to hold his head. "She's got this messianic complex, I tell you. She's appointed herself little mother of all the world. When I found out she had been with Obi I could have killed her. *He* could have killed her. She's going to try to save the world once too often, and she's going to wind up dead."

"My dear boy, your concern is proper and touching." Grundtvig said soothingly. Christian scowled at him. The constant references to his youth seemed to be getting on his nerves. "However," Grundtvig went on, "you have no reason to suppose any danger exists."

"Oh, sure." Christian's voice dripped sarcasm. "She's probably just climbing Mount Everest or looking for the ruins of the sunken continent of Atlantis."

"Possibly." Grundtvig tried to keep his face sober, out of deference to Christian's sensibilities, but the twinkle in his eye betrayed him.

All at once the twinkle faded and Grundtvig said with sudden passion, "Leave her alone, Christian. You don't understand. You are too young. I, who also see the approach of the dying years, the time of failing strength and weakening senses—I understand, and I sometimes wish . . . But there, you will come to it in your turn. Until then take my advice and—"

"Let her kill herself?"

"Yes, if that is her wish! No one else, not even you, has the right to make such a choice for her. But," Grundtvig continued, in a lighter tone, "she won't kill herself, not just yet. She is too clever for that."

Christian rose. "You won't help me, then."

"I have helped. I have given you good advice."

Christian turned on his heel and strode out, without so much as a good-bye. Unperturbed, Grundtvig turned a paternal blue gaze on Elizabeth.

"You are even younger. But you understand, I think."

"I can see both points of view."

"Can you? You are a remarkable young woman. And Christian Rosenberg is a remarkable idiot. Good evening, Miss Elizabeth. I hope we meet again."

III

It took them twenty minutes to find a taxi, and this unremarkable occurrence, which Christian would have taken for granted in Manhattan at rush hour, made him even angrier than he was already.

"I'm going to rent a car, damn it. Should have done it this morning."

Elizabeth made soothing noises. She would have enjoyed the walk if it had not been for Christian's bad humor. The Radhuspladsen, enclosed by handsome old hotels and offices, and faced by the handsome red brick Court House, delighted her tourist's soul. Grundtvig had convinced her there was no need to worry about Margaret, and she was fully prepared to dismiss Christian as a neurotic, domineering son.

In the interests of peace she tried to refrain from references to the interview, but Christian's grumbling finally wore her down and she succumbed to the temptation to needle him.

"Why didn't you tell me about those escapades of Margaret's?"

"You're as big a fool as Grundtvig," Christian said. "This one is different."

"Oh? I suppose masculine intuition tells you so."

But by the time they reached the hotel, Elizabeth was regretting the exchange. Christian was behaving like an idiot, but he was genuinely upset; it was cruel of her to tease him. As they crossed the street she sought for a harmless topic of conversation that would restore them to speaking terms.

"The beggar is gone," she remarked. "I guess he works regular hours like everybody else."

"What beggar?"

"The one you almost knocked down this morning. Didn't you see him? He was right here—"

"There aren't any beggars in Denmark."

"That's silly."

"Well, hardly any." Christian stared intently at the empty spot on the pavement, as if he expected the beggar to rematerialize. "I do vaguely remember someone. It wasn't one of those caterwauling student types?"

"No, he was an older man. Short, shabby, blind."

"There aren't any beggars," Christian repeated. "Social services in Denmark are extensive. They have one of the most advanced . . . Never mind that. Anyhow, this neighborhood is not the sort of place where a beggar would hang out, if there were any beggars."

Elizabeth had no difficulty in following his train of thought.

"For heaven's sake, you're still seeing plots and conspirators," she said in exasperation. "I give up."

Still, she was at Christian's elbow listening more intently that she would have admitted when he asked if there had been any messages. Marie shook her head. She looked tired and harassed.

"I am sorry. It has been such a day—we are a little confused here. Half the staff down with some form of food poisoning, and good workers so hard to find, especially at short notice. I am afraid the kitchen is closed until we locate the source of the trouble."

"What a shame," Elizabeth said sympathetically. "Can we do anything to help?"

Marie laughed. "You would make your own bed, perhaps?"

"I wouldn't mind."

"That is what Margaret would say. Thank you, but I hope we will not have to descend to that."

"Speaking of Margaret," Christian began.

"No, she has not yet returned. But wait, I will see if there is a message. Our receptionist, who is also the telephone operator, was one of those stricken, and the new girl has not yet adjusted to the work. But I will see."

She opened the door in the paneling behind her, and Elizabeth caught a glimpse of an efficient modern office. The blond girl at the switchboard looked up when her employer entered. She did not appear very industrious; though the board in front of her was bright with lights, her hands remained idle as her eyes wandered toward the door, inspecting Christian and Elizabeth with open curiosity.

After taking a few papers from one of the boxes on the wall beside the switchboard, Marie returned, stopping long enough to speak to the girl.

"There were two messages. One was an overseas call—"

"Oh, Lord," Christian muttered. "I'll bet it's Sue. I forgot all about her, and poor old whatever-her-name is, languishing in the hospital. I'd better go see her this evening."

"I'll go with you. I'm ashamed, I should have . . . What's the matter?" For Christian was staring fixedly at the second message. It was a square white envelope without stamp or postmark. The only inscription was his name, Christian Rosenberg, in heavy black block capitals.

"It was delivered by messenger half an hour ago," Marie said. "Is there something wrong, Christian?"

"No." Christian continued to stare at the envelope. "No. Thanks, Marie. No."

She returned to the office. When she had closed the door, Christian ripped the envelope apart. It contained a single sheet of paper. Christian held it in such a way that Elizabeth was unable to read it, but she had a premonition of its import when she saw the blood drain from Christian's face, leaving it as white as the paper he held.

"Oh, no," she whispered. "It can't be—"

"Ah, but it is." Christian's lips turned up in a horrible parody of a smile. "The long-awaited, anxiously anticipated ransom note."

𝓡 4 𝓡

H E STOOD like Lot's wife, staring blankly, until
Elizabeth took his arm and led him into the parlor.
She took the note from his hand.

It contained two paragraphs of writing, in the same anonymous printed capitals. Elizabeth read it. She read it again. Then she raised incredulous eyes to Christian's face.

"This is crazy."

The note read as follows: "The parcel you have misplaced is in our hands. It will be returned to you in exchange for Margaret's bathrobe. Place it or information leading to its whereabouts in a suitcase and leave it on the central bench behind the carousel at Tivoli at a quarter before midnight tonight.

"Do not go to the police. Your visit to them today almost resulted in damage to the parcel. Failure to comply with these instructions will certainly have that effect."

Christian dropped into a chair and held out his hand. "Let me see it again. I was so stunned the first time. . . . " He took his time reading it. "You're right for once," he muttered. "It is crazy. What the hell would anyone want with Margaret's bathrobe?"

"Maybe it's a joke. Would she—"

"Good God, no. She's goofy, but she wouldn't do a cruel thing like this. Let's have a look at that bathrobe."

They crowded into the lift and raced one another through the suite to the armoire in Margaret's room.

"Let me," Elizabeth panted, pushing Christian aside. "I think I remember. . . Yes, here it is."

It was a negligee of shell pink, the yards of flowing silk chiffon trimmed lavishly with maribou feathers. The feathers were molting. They made a dribbling trail across the room as Elizabeth carried the garment to the bed. She ran inquiring hands over it. There were no pockets. The rolled hems on the sleeves and skirt were too narrow to contain even the most minuscule objects. Elizabeth proceeded to squash handful after handful of feathers between her fingers, hoping for a crackle of paper or the feel of something hard. She was left empty-handed except for a coating of feathers that clung maddeningly to her fingers.

"Would you call that a bathrobe?" Christian asked doubtfully. I would call it a negligee. But a man might think of it as a bathrobe. I suppose a man wrote that note?"

"That's a sexist remark."

"There are more male criminals than female."

"Oh, who gives a damn? Look again. I've never seen her wear that ridiculous thing; she must have some other robe."

There was another robe—an ancient terry-cloth garment sadly sagged and carefully mended at the pockets and sleeve. It had once been white.

Elizabeth held it out at arm's length. "It's miles too big for her. It could be a man's robe."

"My father's," Christian said curtly.

"Oh." Elizabeth studied the garment with new respect. "She's mended it, over and over." There were other comments she might have made, but Christian's stony face silenced her. He did not want to wallow in sentimental memories of his father or his mother's fidelity.

"That is most definitely a bathrobe," he said. "And it has more possibilities than the other one. Check the pockets."

Elizabeth did more. She ran her hands over every inch of the robe, inspecting the doubled fabric of collar and cuffs with particular care. The pockets contained two sticks of chewing gum, a handful of tissues, the top off a ball-point pen, and a coupon entitling the possessor to fifteen cents off on a brand of popular instant coffee.

"No luck," she reported.

Christian grunted. Rising, he came to the bed and repeated the inspection. He took an inordinate amount of time doing it. Elizabeth was not offended. She shared his frustration. There had to be something about that robe. . . . Suddenly she was struck with an idea.

"Christian. Your father—was he a hero of the Resistance or some such thing?"

"You could call him that." Christian flung the robe aside. His search, like hers, had produced nothing. "But he was no professional spy or secret agent—nothing like that. Everybody in Denmark was in the Resistance. He couldn't have been involved in anything that would still be active forty years later."

"Schmidt is a German name."

Christian sputtered. "That is the most—I never heard of such a wild, farfetched. . . . where do you get ideas like that, from *Secret Service Comics?"*

"I was just grasping at straws," Elizabeth said humbly.

"I'd grasp at one if I could find one." Christian ran frantic fingers through his hair. "What are we going to do?"

"Give them the robe. What else can we do?"

"Which robe?"

"Both of them. They can have mine too. Maybe they collect bathrobes. Some kind of fetish."

She regretted the feeble witticism as soon as she had uttered it. However, it produced a faint smile from Christian.

"Maybe I should throw mine in as well. Sorry I got so dramatic. It was a shock at first; but now I'm inclined to agree that it must be someone's weird idea of a joke."

"Are you going to do what they ask?"

"Might as well. It can't do any harm." Christian consulted his watch. "But I must go to the hospital; that can't be put off any longer."

"Do you want me to come?"

"I'd rather you stayed here, in case Margaret calls or there are any more messages from psychopaths. Maybe they got their ransom notes mixed up and will send a correction."

II

Christian returned an hour later, looking ruffled and disgruntled. "What a whining little wimp that girl is," he growled.

"That's a terrible thing to say."

"I know, I know. But damn it, she's got the best room in the hospital and round-the-clock nurses; the doctor says it's a clean break and should heal well; and all she can do is cry and say she wants her mother. Which reminds me—I had better call Sue. Have you packed the robes?"

Elizabeth took the hint and retired to her room. She did not particularly want to listen to Christian placating an overprotective mother.

She had already packed the robes, in a brown overnight bag. She had also examined them a third time, using a needle to poke into every possible crevice. She sat down and picked up her guidebook, but found it impossible to concentrate on the splendors of Copenhagen; she was still staring at the first page, seeing nothing of the print, when Christian banged on her door and flung it open without waiting for a response. If there are degrees of disgruntlement, his had risen.

"Ready? Let's go."

"It's not even nine o'clock."

"Do you want to sit around here for three hours chewing your nails? I presume you expect to be fed sometime this evening; we may as well go to one of the restaurants at Tivoli."

When they got downstairs Christian turned aside and opened the door to the office. No one was there except the switchboard operator. She was reading a magazine. Christian's abrupt appearance made her start, but when she saw who it was she relaxed and smiled at him in, Elizabeth thought, a decidedly unbusinesslike fashion.

"Oh, Mr. Rosenberg. You sure made me jump!"

"Any messages?" Christian asked.

"No." The girl shook her head. Bleached blond curls danced and dangling earrings clashed. Elizabeth wondered how she could operate the switchboard without getting things tangled in the wires.

"You did get the other messages, didn't you?" the girl asked.

"Yes, thanks." Christian reached for his wallet. "I'm expecting an important call. You will be especially careful, won't you, to note down any messages that may come for me?"

"Oh, sir, you don't need to do that" But her plump little hand, its nails enameled a nauseating shade of purple, was quick to take the bill he offered. She dimpled and smiled. "I'll be really careful, I promise."

"What an awful accent," Elizabeth said, as they left the lobby. "Cockney or worse. I thought she was Danish."

"They would need someone who spoke English to operate a hotel switchboard," Christian said disinterestedly. "Maybe she was an au pair in England. . . . Damn. I should have had her call for a cab."

"Let's walk. We have plenty of time, and it's a nice night."

It was not a nice night. The sky was overcast, and a chilly breeze made Elizabeth grateful for her white sweater. However, Christian assented with an ill-tempered grunt, and for a while they walked on in silence. Christian kept glancing from side to side, and finally Elizabeth asked, "Are we being followed?"

She meant it as a joke—half a joke, at any rate—but Christian replied seriously, "I'm not sure. Too many people on the street. But I have a feeling. . . . "

"A prickling sensation between the shoulder blades?"

"You seem to be addicted to the most deplorable forms of fiction," Christian said critically. "Where do you dredge up those dreadful clichés?"

However, he was prompt to abandon the quiet side streets for the brightly lit exuberance of Stroget. This thoroughfare, which was admittedly the most direct route to Radhuspladsen and the entrance to Tivoli, was as crowded as it had been earlier, though most of the shops were closed. This time Elizabeth was not distracted by the window displays—Royal Copenhagen porcelain, modern glass, beautiful arrangements of Danish wood and textile design. The brown bag Christian carried was a grim reminder of their mission.

Tivoli cast its famous spell. Walking through the laughter and the light-hearted music, in the glow of a thousand artificial stars, Elizabeth found it hard to believe in danger or kidnappers. The smell of food, wafting from one restaurant after another, reminded her she had not eaten for . . . Good heavens, had it only been five hours? Well, but anxiety is very tiring, she told herself. Frequent replenishment of the vital forces is not only permissible but essential.

Christian strode past one restaurant after another. Elizabeth knew where he was going. She did not protest, though she was sure that a preliminary reconnaissance would satisfy nothing more than idle curiosity.

The carousel circled in a gleaming wonderment of light and color, wrapped in lilting music. They found the benches mentioned in the note without difficulty. There were three of them, facing away from the carousel.

"The place is absolutely teeming with people," Elizabeth said uneasily. "We can't just leave the suitcase and walk away, someone may steal it. Or are Danes more honest than other nationalities?"

"There are hundreds of other nationalities here," was Christian's reply. "But there won't be so many of them at eleven forty-five. The gardens close at midnight."

So the chosen spot made reasonably good sense after all, Elizabeth realized. Most of the children, who were the best customers of the carousel, would be home in bed by the time specified, and if the gardens closed at midnight, some visitors would have begun drifting toward the entrance.

"I suppose you intend to lurk in the shadows and see who collects the suitcase," she said.

"The notion had passed through my mind."

"It won't work."

"What do you mean, it won't work? Why won't it?"

"If this isn't a joke—if some demented character really does yearn to posses those dreadful bathrobes—he'll expect you to watch for him. He'll create a distraction to prevent you from seeing him."

"Like how?"

"Like hitting you over the head—or worse—before he goes anywhere near the suitcase." Suddenly Elizabeth was furious. She clenched her fists. "What do you think you're doing? What's come over you? This isn't your style. You're a stockbroker, not a private eye."

"Now, Beth—"

"Don't call me that!"

"Betsy? Liz?"

"My name is Elizabeth. I hate nicknames. Shall I call you Chris?"

"You can if you like."

Instead of turning away her wrath, the soft answer made her even angrier. She shook his arm. "I know what you're thinking. You can just stop thinking it."

"How do you know what—"

"You're planning to get rid of me." She continued to tug at his sleeve, like a small angry dog. "You're going to stuff me full of food, and shove me into a taxi, and tell me to go to the hotel. I won't go. You can't make me."

"I could," Christian said softly. "There are ways."

They glowered at one another for a few moments. Then, spontaneously and simultaneously, they both began to laugh.

"Shades of Philip Marlowe and James Bond," Elizabeth gasped. "What kind of deplorable fiction have *you* been reading, Mr. Rosenberg?"

Christian shook his head. "I can't believe what I just said. It must be Margaret's influence. Craftily, insidiously, her nuttiness eventually poisons everyone who associates with her. Let's get something to eat and discuss the situation in a calm, rational manner."

They found a table in an open-air pavilion, so they could watch the passersby. Not, as Christian admitted, that they would know a villain if they saw one; the only suspects they had actually set eyes on were the enigmatic Mr. Schmidt and the extremely unmemorable little man with the trunk. But, as Christian pointed out, you never knew.

"We are in a singularly vulnerable position," he said. "They know us but we don't know them. We're understaffed, that's one of our problems."

"Maybe we should have gone to the police."

"They told us not to."

"And how do you suppose they knew we had been at police headquarters this afternoon?"

Christian stabbed a fork into his fish with such vehemence that flakes flew all over the table. "Obviously they've been following us. Someone is probably watching us right now."

The idea struck both of them at the same moment. With a precision suggestive of long rehearsals, they dived under the table, hitting their heads painfully together.

"Ow," Elizabeth gasped, clutching her brow.

"It's still there," Christian croaked, clutching his.

"But that would be clever of them—telling us to put the suitcase on the bench at a particular hour, and then snatching it when we weren't expecting trouble."

"Apparently they aren't that clever."

"This isn't over yet. I think," Elizabeth said nervously, "that I would like another glass of beer."

"You've already had three."

"Who's counting?"

"I am. If you don't stay sober I will stuff you into a taxi. You'll be too drunk to resist."

They did have another glass of beer—Christian absentmindedly ordered one for himself, and actually drank it—and then coffee, and then more beer, in order to have an excuse to stay where they were until the witching hour arrived. Christian was sitting on the suitcase. It was a very uncomfortable cushion, and his sudden spurt in height had astonished the waiter; but there was no denying that a thief would have a hard time abstracting it from that position without attracting attention. Among the strolling crowds theft would be much easier.

Elizabeth's watch was behaving strangely. Sometimes the hands scarcely seemed to move; then they would leap forward, a quarter of an hour at a time. As eleven o'clock neared and then passed, her internal mechanisms also started to function erratically, speeding up her heartbeat and her breathing, causing her to perspire one moment and shiver the next. On the whole, it was a relief when her watch finally read eleven thirty.

"Shall we?" she asked.

Christian had been concentrating on his own watch. "Let's," he said.

The next ten minutes were the worst of all. Christian clutched the suitcase with both arms. Elizabeth trotted close beside him. Both rolled their eyes wildly from side to side. They reached the carousel without incident and stopped at a discreet distance from the designated bench.

"Somebody's there,"Christian exclaimed.

"Who? Where?" His broad shoulders and extended elbows obscured Elizabeth's view. She craned to look.

The huddled form might have been male or female. A bulky coat obscured its shape, and its face was hidden by a broad-brimmed hat pulled down over its brow. Then the person sat up, and she saw an elderly gentleman, eyes slitted with sleepiness, mouth concealed by an enormous white mustache.

"He looks innocent enough," she muttered.

"That is an incredibly naive remark, even for you. There is, as you yourself pointed out, the risk of theft. They could eliminate that risk if they had a man on the spot, waiting for delivery."

"As conspicuously as that? We'd recognize him if we saw him again."

"Would we? That's a fake mustache if ever I saw one."

Elizabeth pivoted slowly till they stood back to back. "I don't see any suspicious characters."

"Keep looking." He let out a yelp and jumped aside as a heavily bearded youth in dungarees and a T-shirt inscribed with an obscene suggestion reeled toward him.

The youth looked at him in surprise, remarked, "Hey, man, stay cool," and staggered past.

"Sorry," Christina said, wiping his brow.

"I'm nervous too. For God's sake, put the damned suitcase on the bench. It must be eleven forty-five."

"Five more minutes. Keep looking, will you?"

"I'm looking, I'm looking."

The carousel started on another of its purposeless circuits. The gleaming snow-white horses swung into motion; the gray elephant, trunk lifted, seemed to shift its heavy feet. As she watched, Elizabeth was overcome, suddenly and without warning, by a shocking suffusion of frustrated anger.

There was an old saying—something along the lines of "God always answers prayers—but not the way you expect." Or maybe it went, "If God does answer your prayer you'll probably wish He hadn't." She had prayed and her prayer had been answered; and God must be a comedian, just as she had sometimes suspected He was, for her entrée into Margaret Rosenberg's charmed circle had brought her nothing but grief. If she had arrived as a simple tourist, unaccompanied and uncommitted, by this time she would have found a friend—a cheerful, witty Danish student or teacher—or businessman or ditch digger—anybody, as long as he wasn't a pompous snob with a crazy mother. He would take her to see the Little Mermaid and the Changing of the Guard at the royal palace, and he would ride on the merry-go-round with her, side by side on paired white horses, holding her hand and laughing.

She was ashamed of her anger, failing to recognize it for what it was—a not unusual accompaniment to tension and worry—but it continued to bubble and seethe as her wistful eyes followed the circling animals and her foot unconsciously beat time to the music. There were adults on the carousel now— a young couple in jeans and matching shirts, shrieking with laughter; a group of girls whose long fair hair lifted in rhythm to the movement of their mounts; a bedizened hussy whose legs were too chubby to be displayed in black net stockings, her skirt slit clear up to ...

She sat sidesaddle on the giraffe, her feet dangling. Her shoes had six-inch heels, and they were completely coated with rhinestones, heels and all. An enormous black silk shawl, fringed and sequined, enveloped her torso, and dark glasses covered most of her face, from her platinum hair to her bright-red cheeks. Carried away by the rapture of the ride, she had allowed her mouth to open in a blissful grin. The teeth were unmistakable, and nothing less than a thick piece of blanket could have hidden the nose.

Elizabeth, mute with disbelief, jabbed Christian hard in the ribs. He jumped a good three inches and let out a high-pitched shriek, but—let it be said to his credit—he did not relax his grip on the suitcase. Before he could express the emotion that crimsoned his face, Elizabeth jabbed him again. "Look, look—it's her!"

She was to blush over this grammatical slip later, but at the time grammar was the least of her worries. In tones of mounting hysteria she repeated, "It's her, it's Margaret— there, you dolt—on the carousel."

Christian was slow to respond. By the time he focused his eyes the giraffe was passing out of sight.

"What are you talking about?" he demanded. "Where?"

"On the giraffe. Wait for it."

The next circuit found them ready and watching. At the sight of the incredible little figure Christian made the sort of sound produced by people who have been punched hard in the stomach. Margaret had seen them. Her mouth was open and her lips moved, in slow, exaggerated shapings. The giraffe moved serenely past.

"Bathrobe," Elizabeth exclaimed. "Didn't she say bathrobe?"

Christian bounded forward, then back. For a brief period he vibrated from one foot to the other, like a poorly managed puppet. "Bathrobe," he babbled. "Is that what . . . I don't know. I can't decide. . . . Get her off there. The suitcase . . . "

"She wants us to deliver the suitcase." Elizabeth hazarded a guess. "Quick, put it on the bench. Then we'll grab her."

The giraffe reappeared. Margaret had lost interest in them. Hand shading her eyes—Cortez (in drag) surveying the Pacific from a peak in Darien—she appeared to be searching for something.

With a convulsive movement Christian tossed the suitcase in the general direction of the bench. By a miracle it landed in the right place. The bench was now unoccupied. The mustachioed gentleman had left.

The giraffe came around again. Margaret was still peering intently at the crowd.

Christian shuddered. "Did you say something about a distraction?" he asked feebly.

He didn't know the half of it. He had barely finished speaking when the genuine distraction began—an explosion of crackling sound and a burst of rainbow stars streaming down from the aery vault of heaven. The famed fireworks of Tivoli were right on schedule

It was too much for Elizabeth. The suitcase, the carousel, Margaret, the old gentleman with the mustache, the fireworks . . . she fought an urgent desire to sit down on the ground and relegate all of the above, except the fireworks, to the nethermost pits.

Margaret came around again. Extreme agitation distorted her face. She pointed at something. The bench?

Christian ran toward the carousel. Elizabeth stayed where she was. She had never been so confused.

Obviously Margaret had not been kidnapped at all. There she was, circling slowly on a giraffe. The threat was false, the danger nonexistent. That was a relief, and very pleasant to know, but it did not alter the fact that some person or persons unknown had played a nasty trick on Christian. For all its elements of insane fantasy, the ransom note had sounded serious. It might be a good idea to find out who wanted Margaret's bathrobe.

Elizabeth decided she could safely leave the repossession of Margaret to her son. He wasn't going to reach her for a while, though. The carousel continued to whirl, bleating out its cheery tune, and the attendant seemed to be holding his own in his struggle to prevent Christian from mounting it. Elizabeth turned her attention to the suitcase.

At least she tried to. The fireworks were not merely a distraction; they overwhelmed every sense. Showers of golden light, bursts of shining crimson and emerald stars, silver fountains leaping into the blue-velvet darkness. . . . In one glare of light Elizabeth saw the man with the mustache. With a number of other spectators he was watching the fireworks, his head tilted back, his mouth agape. He was just as innocent and harmless as she had supposed. The suitcase lay where Christian had tossed it. No one was paying the slightest attention to it.

She risked a quick glance over her shoulder and was glad to see that Christian had given up his attempt to force his way onto the carousel. He stood with his back to her, his head moving to follow his mother's circling form.

As the giraffe passed again, Margaret raised her arm and hurled a missile that struck her son full in the face. He staggered. The carousel started to slow down. Out of nowhere a form appeared, bearing down on Christian with the slow deliberation of a trotting buffalo. It was the form of a very large man wearing a knitted cap. For a moment Christian's form was blotted out; then the very large man proceeded on his inexorable path, leaving Christian sitting on the grass. The carousel ground to a stop. A final climatic explosion of colored stars rained down from the heavens.

Elizabeth turned. The suitcase was gone.

In a leisurely fashion she strolled toward her fallen associate. She noted, in passing, that the giraffe's saddle was empty.

Christian's face was covered with streams of gory liquid.

"An apple?" Elizabeth inquired.

"Plum," Christian said thickly.

"We may as well go home."

"Why not?" Christian allowed her to assist him to rise. "You see what I mean?" he asked.

Elizabeth nodded. She saw what he meant.

⚜ 5 ⚜

THE CAROUSEL spun faster and faster. White horses, golden giraffes, gray elephants blended into a blur of color. One by one the animals detached and flew off into space, carrying their riders with them: Margaret, dressed like Groucho Marx, with a painted black mustache; Chief Grundtvig, in Santa Claus suit, beaming and waving; Christian, wearing top hat and tails, rigid, scowling.

Elizabeth awoke with a start and glanced at the clock on the bedside table. She relaxed with a sigh of relief. Six thirty. She had not overslept.

The plum that burst on Christian's brow had contained a note. The paper was extremely sticky. By the time Christian untangled the folds and creases, only a part of the message was legible: "Radhus . . . Eight (8)." The writing straggled too wildly to be identifiable as Margaret's, but it certainly resembled the penmanship of someone who had written it while riding on a giraffe.

So they would be at Radhuspladsen at eight o'clock. And where that would lead them, only God and Margaret knew.

Elizabeth was not anxious to get up. Christian had been in a grisly mood the previous night, and there was no reason to suppose he would be any more affable this morning. With a sigh she flung back the covers and prepared to face a dismal and confusing day.

She brushed her teeth with punctilious attention to each and every molar and applied her makeup with as much care as if she were preparing for an audience at the palace. Then, as she realized why she was dawdling, she stamped her foot and swore. Damn Christian Rosenberg anyway. She was not going to be intimidated by his rotten moods, and she was sick and tired of chasing his crazy mother. She wanted to see the Little Mermaid.

In this belligerent mood she burst into the sitting room to find that Christian was up, dressed, and talking on the telephone. When she appeared he gestured toward the table and went on talking.

Elizabeth poured coffee and listened to the conversation. It was short and not very sweet. "You haven't? Well, if she gets in touch with you, please let me know."

Christian hung up. He consulted a small leatherbound book and dialed again.

"How many people have you called?" Elizabeth asked.

"Eight. Six of them were . . . Hello? Is this the residence of Madame Brunner?" A pained expression crossed his face and he listened for a while in silence. "Well, I'm sorry," he said. "I didn't—Hello? Hello?"

"Six of them were still asleep?" Elizabeth said. "Not to mention Madame Brunner. Christian, it's only seven A.M. You can't call people at this hour."

"She's out of town," Christian muttered. "Madame. That was her butler. What a foul mouth that man has!"

"So you're calling Margaret's friends."

"Yes."

"Isn't that rather futile?"

"Probably."

"Christian—what would happen if we didn't go to Radhuspladsen this morning?"

Christian shrugged wearily. "Damned if I know."

"The ransom note was a fake," Elizabeth argued. "Margaret isn't a prisoner; she's alive and well and free as a cuckoo bird. I mean, really, Christian, if this is a mystery story, it's the most insipid one I've ever run into. No bodies, no blood, no murderous attacks—"

"You seem to have forgotten that unfortunate girl in the hospital," Christian snapped. He added petulantly, "I never can remember her name."

The reminder silenced Elizabeth. Christian hammered the point home. "I admit this is a singularly bloodless little caper so far; but that doesn't mean the element of danger is lacking. Efficient crooks don't slaughter people indiscriminately. Evidently they have not needed to damage anyone except— er—"

"Marian."

"Yeah."

"I'm tired of chasing aimlessly around town," Elizabeth complained. "If I knew why—"

"What would you rather be doing? No, don't tell me— going to see the Little Mermaid."

"This was supposed to be my vacation."

"All right, have your damned vacation! Go sightseeing, visit museums, take tours. See if I care."

"I can't."

"Why the hell not?"

Elizabeth slammed her fist down on the table. "Ouch," she said. "Because, much as I hate to admit it, you have a point. One possible explanation for all this—this insanity—is that Margaret has something, or knows something, that certain other people want. The attack on—er—Marian at the airport was designed to give them—the gang, I guess we have to call them—access to Margaret. I don't know what the bathrobe has to do with it, and I can't imagine why she is running aimlessly around Copenhagen instead of going to the police—"

"Oh, I know why she's doing that," Christian said. "She loves playing detective. The police wouldn't let her play."

"She wouldn't. . . . Yes, I guess she would. Has it occurred to you that maybe she has done something illegal?"

"Yes, it has. It has also occurred to me that she may be running away from someone who means her harm. Why do you think I'm so anxious to corral her?"

"All right." Elizabeth picked up her purse. "Let's go."

"Radhuspladsen?"

"Radhuspladsen."

II

The town square of Copenhagen covers an area of several blocks. It is not the most specific of all meeting places. Standing somewhere near the center of the vast paved expanse, Elizabeth scanned the faces that passed in a never-ending procession.

"This is hopeless. How are we supposed to find her here?"

"Keep looking." Christian turned slowly on his axis.

The view was distracting. On the west corner of the square was a dramatic fountain whose sculptures depicted a bull and a dragon in furious combat. A column nearby supported two giant statues of green (formerly copper) men blowing giant horns. The clock on the tower of the Town Hall said eight thirty. They had been wandering aimlessly around the square for forty minutes.

Elizabeth nudged Christian and indicated a group of tables clustered around a kiosk on the east side of the area.

"I want a cup of coffee. If you're too stubborn to admit this is a lost cause, let's at least sit down."

Christian assented unenthusiastically. "We can see, and be seen, just as well from there, I guess."

As the hands of the clock moved to nine, and then to five minutes past the hour, Christian's shoulders sagged lower. Elizabeth was neither disappointed nor disheartened. She hadn't expected Margaret would show up. In fact, she rather doubted that the note in the plum had been meant for Christian. If Margaret had intended to throw it to him, she probably would have missed him by a mile. She had appeared to be looking for someone in the crowd. And if she knew Christian had intercepted a message intended for that person, she would be careful to stay away.

If, if, if! Elizabeth fully sympathized with Christian's exasperation with his mother. Margaret moved through life in a fog of hypotheses, creating one unlikely situation after another.

Brooding thus, her eyes absently watching the passing traffic, she suddenly bounded to her feet with a shriek. Christian might reasonably have asked what the devil was wrong with her. Instead he stared in the direction indicated by her rigid, pointing forefinger, and he was in time to see what had prompted her cry.

A large red tourist bus moved past, slowed by the heavy morning traffic. Peering interestedly out of one of the windows was the face of a dear little old lady wearing granny glasses and a black dress with crocheted collar and cuffs. Her fluffy white hair was crowned by an object—one hesitated to call it a hat—like a giant pink cabbage, from which two hat pins protruded, crossing six inches above the hat in the manner of chopsticks.

Secure in this disguise, which was completed by a camera pressed against the window glass, the woman gazed serenely out until her wandering eye met Elizabeth's. She gave a violent start. The pink cabbage slid drunkenly to one side and the spectacles tobogganed toward the tip of her nose. Her lips shaped a silent word. It began with a *d* and ended with an *n*. Then the traffic began to move, and her look of alarm turned into a broad smile, brimming with teeth. Raising the camera, she took their picture. The bus roared off.

"Wait, wait," Elizabeth screamed, as Christian gathered himself for pursuit. "You can't chase a bus through the streets."

"God *damn* that woman," Christian said passionately. "She did that on purpose. We've got to find out where the bus is going."

"How?"

"It was red," Christian said. The inadequacy of this description struck him as soon as he uttered it; his fair cheeks darkened. "For God's sake, didn't you notice anything about it? License number, a name—anything?"

Elizabeth ignored the injustice of the demand. This was no time for petty personal exchanges. She tried to concentrate. Finally she said, "It was a tourist bus—not one of the regular city buses. And I think I saw the word 'Viking.'"

"Half the objects in this city, stationary and mobile, have the word 'Viking' on them," Christian grumbled. "Well, that's something. Let's look for tourist companies."

Elizabeth suspected that by the time they completed such an inquiry the bus would have become untraceable. But she did not demur; Christian's temper required action, however futile. If he had had to sit still he would have burst.

Frenzied interrogation of a policeman and a hotel porter produced the information that many bus tours started from Radhuspladsen, and that there was indeed a company named Viking. They proceeded to the office of this organization, which was not far away. Here Christian's increasingly fluent Danish, which seemed to flow from subconscious depths when necessity required it, won the sympathy of a pretty young woman, who told them the bus was probably their Vikingland tour, which had left the square at the specified time. Upon hearing this, Christian gritted his teeth.

"She boarded that bus not a hundred yards from where we were sitting. She must have seen us. When I get my hands on her . . ."He turned back to the helpful young woman. Elizabeth didn't understand what he said, but deduced, from the shocked pity on the girl's face, that he had invented a story as tragic as it was untrue. She produced a folder describing the tour and a map showing the route of the bus.

Thus far Christian's performance had been impressive. His next move left Elizabeth rapt with admiration.

"Let's pick up the car."

"What car?"

"I told you I planned to rent one."

"Yes, but . . . " Elizabeth's breath gave out. Holding her by the wrist, like a large reluctant dog by the leash, he was towing her along at a speed that made her legs ache.

"I asked Roger to take care of it for me this morning," Christian explained. "He knew of a place just off Radhuspladsen. They should have it ready for us."

He sounded extremely smug. For once Elizabeth didn't blame him.

The car was ready, and the formalities were concluded in a surprisingly short time. When Christian guided the vehicle into the teeming traffic, Elizabeth saw by the clock on the tower that barely an hour had passed since they saw Margaret on the bus. She buckled her seat belt. Christian's lowering brow and white-knuckled grip on the wheel portended a rough ride.

She didn't venture to speak to him until they had left the drab western suburbs behind and were pelting along a wide superhighway.

"Where are we going?" she asked.

"Roskilde. Didn't you hear what that girl said?"

"I didn't understand a word. Besides," Elizabeth went on, promptly contradicting herself, "that bus stops at half a dozen places. We're an hour behind—"

"We're going directly to Roskilde. The bus winds all over the countryside, giving the tourists their money's worth of quaint villages and thatched cottages. Hopefully we'll catch up with Margaret at the Cathedral."

"But the bus goes to the Viking Ship museum and farm and a couple of other places."

"How do you know that? I thought you didn't understand what the girl said."

"I have read every brochure put out by every travel agency in Denmark. I had my entire itinerary planned six weeks ago. After I had seen the Little Mermaid I was going to—"

"Will you kindly stick to the point, if you have one?"

"The point," Elizabeth said, through clenched teeth, "is that Margaret may be heading for one of the other places on the tour. Besides, she knows we saw her. If she has any sense she'll ditch the tour at the first opportunity."

"That's a chance we'll have to take. I don't know what she is doing on that bus, but presumably she is not simply passing time. If there is any method in her madness—which I am not prepared to swear to—there may be something, at one of those stops, that will give us a clue. You're the professional tourist; haven't you any ideas?"

Elizabeth picked up the brochure and opened it.

" 'Two Country Rhapsody,' " she read aloud. " 'See the best of Denmark and Sweden. At Elsinore, the narrowest point between the two countries . . . ' That was one of the things I wanted to see—a performance of *Hamlet,* at—"

"Stop drooling," Christian said vulgarly. "That's the wrong tour."

Reluctantly Elizabeth passed over the Afternoon Hamlet tour, the Royal Tour of Copenhagen, and the Castle Tour of North Zealand. "Here it is. The Vikingland Tour. 'This tour visits a four-thousand-year-old passage grave at Om. Afterwards we proceed to the old city of Roskilde, in ancient times the capital of Denmark. In the great Roskilde Cathedral there are thirty-seven royal tombs. Lunch at two-hundred-years-old thatched inn (not included in the fare) . . . ' They never include lunch. I think that's rotten. People may not want—"

Christian cut her off. "Any ideas?"

"No," Elizabeth admitted. "It's a little hard to reason logically when you haven't a clue to start with. Wait a minute. I have my guidebook."

"You would."

"I always carry it." Elizabeth saw no reason to add that she had decided to take in as many sights as possible while they continued their pointless pursuit. "Maybe it will suggest something."

She read Christian a long, interesting paragraph about passage tombs, the burial places of the prehistoric inhabitants of Denmark. He refused to be interested.

"This is a waste of time."

"Shut up and listen. We're groping in the dark anyway." Elizabeth turned pages. "Roskilde. The eight-hundred-year-old Domkirke, or Cathedral, is the St. Denis of Denmark, containing the tombs of thirty-seven Danish monarchs, from Margaret the First to—"

"Hold it. What did you just say?"

"From Margaret the First to. . . . You really are grasping at straws, Christian. I thought you had decided that the biography of Queen Margaret was a pretense."

"It's the first connection we've found."

"Christian, either your mother is fleeing in terror from an anonymous bunch of criminals, or she is doing research for her book. She can't be doing both. In the latter case there might conceivably be some reason for her to visit Margaret's tomb, but why would she take a tourist bus?"

"She's probably planning to dig up the body," Christian growled.

Elizabeth started to laugh. A glance at Christian's grim visage made her change her mind.

"She hates to drive," he went on seriously. "A sensible woman would have hired a car or taken the train, but that isn't Margaret's style. She probably thought this was a cute way of getting where she wanted to go."

"Then she'll leave the tour at Roskilde—not go back with the rest of them."

"No, I can't see her doing that. Those poor devils of tour guides have to account for every warm body at every stop. Margaret is crazy about tours; she's dragged me on several. I remember how indignant she was once, when we went to Kenilworth Castle or some such ruin, and two of the passengers didn't get back to the bus at the designated time. The other passengers were bitching at the guide and the guide was having nervous palpitations. No, she wouldn't do that unless she was desperate. I'm inclined to think that if she is going to Roskilde for a specific purpose, it's something that can be accomplished in a very short time—maybe only a few minutes. They don't give you much time on these whirlwind tours."

"Then she can't be planning to dig up Margaret's remains," Elizabeth said, with a sidelong glance at her companion.

"That's right." Christian's dour expression lightened a trifle. "Those monuments are solid stone, aren't they? And in broad daylight, with people all around. . . . Are you laughing? What the hell are you laughing about?"

Elizabeth was incapable of replying. Every time she tried to conquer her amusement, Christian's astonished and affronted face set her off again.

The rest of the drive passed in silence. Elizabeth alternately read her guidebook—it would not be wise, she decided, to read aloud—and gazed out the window. She thought longingly of the bus tour, slowly wheezing along lovely country lanes, past quaint old villages and houses with thatched roofs. The highway was dull. The scenery was dull—gently rolling, green with summer crops, but dull. The weather was dull. Clouds hid the sun and an occasional spatter of rain spotted the windshield. Dullest of all was her companion.

Like most tourist towns, the quaint part of Roskilde is limited to a small section in the center—the old city. The suburbs looked like any other town in any country, except that the street and shop signs were in Danish. Then they rounded a curve and Roskilde Domkirke came into view, raising powerful importunate arms toward the threatening sky. It wasn't Chartres or Rheims, but it had a grave dignity of its own; and Elizabeth let out a yelp of disappointment when Christian turned away from it, onto a side street.

"I thought we were going—"

"There it is!" Christian swung the wheel and turned into a parking lot. "That's the one, isn't it?"

"I guess so." There were a dozen buses in the lot, but only one of them was red. "It looks like the same one."

"Then the group must be at the Cathedral right now." Christian chuckled fiendishly.

A gentle drizzling rain began to fall as they ascended the sloping walk leading up to the hill from which the Cathedral commanded the city. The wet sidewalks and the crowds of visitors made walking difficult. When Elizabeth paused to tie a transparent rain hat over her hair, Christian forged ahead. She caught up with him at the entrance. He frowned at her.

"No stopping to look at the view. This is serious business."

He did not wait for her angry rebuttal, but darted into the vestry, where a counter displaying postcards and guidebooks caught Elizabeth's attention. She decided she had better not try it; but an indignant guard caught Christian at the inner door, demanding tickets, and while he was buying them Elizabeth acquired a guidebook with lovely color photographs. She was not given time to peruse it. Christian handed over the tickets and went in, herding her ahead of him.

The interior was pleasing mixture of Romanesque and early Gothic. The tall piers were adorned, for the most part, only by sections of white paint that contrasted handsomely with the rich red brick of the unpainted portions. The main aisle was relatively deserted. A single glance told them that their quarry was not in sight.

This left them with something of a problem, however, since the church was vast, and its chief attraction seemed to be the series of chapels containing the royal tombs, on both sides of the central structure. Elizabeth pointed this out, referring ostentatiously to her guidebook.

"You go right, I'll go left," Christian said. "We'll meet by the high altar. And no sightseeing!"

This was tantamount to ushering an alcoholic into a well-stocked bar and ordering him not to sample the wares; but Elizabeth summoned up all her willpower and succeeded fairly well. The charming faded frescoes on the white vault of the first chapel she entered tested her strength to the uttermost, but after an anguished glance at twining vines and flowers and graceful portraits of bishops, saints, and martyrs, she turned her attention to the much less attractive forms of the tourists who were examining the Renaissnce marble monuments to two early monarchs—presumably a Christian and a Frederick, since all Danish kings since 1425 have borne one name or the other. Several of the female tourists were oddly dressed; one overweight woman had forced her curves into an ensemble of black leather tunic, pants, and boots. But none of them was Margaret.

The next chapel was exquisitely, whitely neoclassical. Elizabeth let out a muffled bleat of anguish, but doggedly stuck to her mission. In and out among the tombs, peering behind columns and into alcoves, constantly wheeling and whirling to make sure her quarry had not slipped past her, she finally reached the end of the nave. Christian was waiting, rolling his eyes from side to side and rotating slowly, like a figure atop a music box.

"No luck?" he asked, continuing to revolve. "The choir is the only place left, then."

"Queen Margaret's tomb is behind the altar," said Elizabeth, who had snatched a look at the guidebook.

"Oh? We'll converge on it. Pincer movement. You go—"

"Right."

As she proceeded, Elizabeth's interest in the living Margaret was momentarily eclipsed by curiosity about her long-dead namesake. This was her first chance to see what the legendary lady had looked like. The guidebook contained a photograph of the marble effigy atop the tomb. It was a lovely profile—idealized, almost certainly, for Margaret had died nastily of plague at the age of almost sixty. Yet the carving had captured the royal lady's indomitable spirit.

Many of the older monuments were in this part of the church, and a majority of the sightseers had gathered there. Margaret's tomb, a high marble platform with sculptured figures along the sides, was virtually hidden by the bodies of the curious. The voices of half a dozen guides, lecturing in as many languages, blended in a distracting mumble.

Elizabeth edged toward the tomb. Yes, by heaven, there it was—a flash of pink cabbage leaves. Only a flash; Margaret was short, and it was easy for her to conceal herself amount taller bodies.

On the far side of the choir stood Christian, his eyes moving over the crowd. Apparently he hadn't seen his mother. There were a number of people between them, including one very large man in a shabby navy-blue coat, with a knitted cap pulled down over...

Elizabeth rose to her tiptoes and waved frantically. Christian saw her. So did a number of other people, including the very large man in the knitted cap.

His face was as deeply tanned as an Indian's, but his features and a pair of blue eyes so pale they resembled faded marbles suggested that he was a native of the northern peninsula, if not Denmark itself. When the milky-blue eyes focused on Elizabeth they bulged alarmingly. His mouth opened. Over the discreet murmurs of the lecturing guides sounded a high tenor howl of alarm or fury. This sound was joined by a swelling chorus of shrieks and shouts as he turned and forced his way through the throng, sweeping people aside with flailing movements of his arms.

Christian could have avoided him. Instead he stepped forward and raised one hand in a magisterial gesture. Elizabeth saw his lips shape a few words—she thought they were, "Now, see here, you"—before a horizontal navy-blue object obscured his face and sent him reeling into a tomb. The very large man was now moving at a ponderous run, like an antique train engine getting up steam. Elizabeth caught a last fleeting glimpse of his face as he headed down the side aisle. Tears streamed from his eyes. Sobbing noisily, he moved into full throttle and disappeared behind a pier.

The pink cabbage had, of course, also disappeared. Its very conspicuousness had advantages; Margaret had only to remove it to blend with the crowd.

Elizabeth picked her way fastidiously through the fallen bodies to where Christian was squatting, head bowed, knuckles resting on the floor in orangutang fashion. He shook his head dizzily. A surrealist spatter of red drops speckled the marble.

"Put your head back," Elizabeth suggested, offering him a handful of tissues.

Christian disdained this gift in favor of his own handkerchief. He was the only man Elizabeth had ever known who always had a large, clean white handkerchief. She had to admit that on this occasion its usefulness was unquestionable. His nose was bleeding with copious abandon.

No one paid any attention to them. Christian was only one of a number of victims, and as attendants and fellow tourists ran to assist the fallen, they withdrew into a convenient alcove.

"Oofaher," Christian said, through the bloody wad of linen.

"What?"

"Look for her. I'll go left, you go—"

"Oh, don't be silly. She's long gone. That man over there seems to be a doctor; maybe he can help stop—"

"It's stopped."

"Then go wash your face. You look terrible."

"No time," Christian mumbled. "Got to hurry."

"Where?"

"Back to the bus."

"You don't think she would be stupid enough to go there, do you?"

"It's worth a try "

It had stopped raining, but the walks were slippery with water and Christian, still a trifle dazed, allowed Elizabeth to set a moderate pace.

"We know what one of the gang looks like now; that's one thing gained," she said brightly.

Christian growled.

"It was the same man who was at Tivoli last night," she went on. "That can't be coincidence. And he's certainly distinctive looking. I'd say he's at least six feet six inches tall."

"At least," Christian mumbled. "That's the second time he's knocked me down." He rubbed his arm and grimaced.

"Oh, I don't think he has anything personal against you," Elizabeth said consolingly. "He knocked a lot of other people down too. I must say it wasn't very bright of you to get in his way. If I saw a creature that size coming at me . . . What's the matter?"

Christian stopped walking. He put his hand inside his jacket, Napoleon style, and then Elizabeth was treated to the strange spectacle of a bare finger sticking out of his shoulder. The phenomenon was so unusual that it took her a few seconds to connect the effect with the obvious cause.

The finger was protruding through a hole in Christian's sleeve. It was a symmetrical round hole, so neat in shape that it could only have been made by a finically tidy moth—or by a bullet.

🐝 6 🐝

CHRISTIAN removed his finger from the hole and his arm from the sleeve of his jacket. A ragged tear, surrounded by a narrow rim of blood, marked his shirt sleeve just below the shoulder.

"Oh, my goodness," Elizabeth said feebly.

"Grazed me," Christian said. "Close, but no cigar. Yes, here's the exit hole. Lucky the sleeve is loose."

"Are you all right?" Elizabeth asked.

"Just a scratch," Christian said, with studied nonchalance. He squared his shoulders and attempted, with some success, to look as if being shot at was an everyday occurrence in his adventurous life. "I didn't hear a shot. A silencer, I suppose." He laughed lightly.

"Oh, my goodness," Elizabeth repeated, even more feebly. She swayed. But Christian was through playing hero. Instead of putting a protective arm around her and pressing her to his manly chest, he grinned malevolently.

"That'll learn you. A bloodless little plot, did you say? No violence, did you say? Ha! Who was right and who was wrong, Miss Know-it-all?"

"You were right and I was wrong," Elizabeth murmured.

"Now let's go to the bus."

Elizabeth followed at a respectful distance. She had a feeling that this new Christian was going to be even more trying to live with than the stodgy stockbroker.

II

People were pouring out of the Cathedral and along the walk. Elizabeth overheard a number of references to what had happened, some indignant and shocked, some amused and curious. The guides were hurrying their charges away as expeditiously as possible. This sort of thing wasn't good for tourism.

The passengers who belonged to the red Vikingland bus were climbing on board when Elizabeth and Christian reached the parking lot. Christian started to get on, then changed his mind and engaged the driver in conversation. Turning to Elizabeth, he reported, "He remembers her."

"Who wouldn't?"

"He says she hasn't come back yet."

"If we are going to lurk in waiting, I suggest we get out of sight."

"Good idea," Christian said patronizingly. He withdrew behind the bus.

A few last stragglers got on. The bus appeared to be full, but the driver was still outside, smoking a leisurely cigarette.

"What are they waiting for?" Elizabeth asked.

"The guide, probably. He or she would be the last one on."

Finally they caught sight of her—a lean, gray-haired woman whose expression, a blend of anxious smile and worried frown, betokened her profession. Leaning heavily on her arm was another woman approximately twice her bulk and about her own age. The latter was obviously American. Her strident tones, redolent of the Midwestern heartland, floated to Elizabeth's ears.

"Outrageous...scandalous...sue the bus company... sue you....sue Denmark...."

"But, madame," the guide gasped, staggering under the complainant's weight, "the doctor said there was no injury; you are not hurt; I regret the shock and inconvenience, but you cannot blame the company."

The pair came to a halt by the steps of the bus. The large irate female bared her arm. It was muscled like that of a boxer, and bore a number of bruises, most of them fading. She indicated one, about an inch in diameter.

"Not hurt? My arm is probably broken. I feel extreme mental anguish. The shock!" She clutched her expansive bosom. "Such a thing could never have happened in a well-regulated country. Back home we—"

"Have the highest crime rate in the civilized world," Christian said, stepping forward. "Why don't you get on the bus, lady, and stop slandering a really civilized nation?"

"How dare you! I'll report you, young man; what right have you—"

"I work for Interpol," Christian said. Elizabeth gasped. He scowled warningly at her and continued, "We got a tip from a snitch that a drug drop was going down at the Cathedral. You better come along with me, lady."

The woman's reply was essentially unintelligible. It consisted mainly of gasps and snorts and cries of protest. Christian finally let her get on the bus, which she was more than ready to do. Then he turned to the guide.

She shrank back. "Oh, sir, you do not suspect me! I am an honest woman; I work for my living."

Christian had the grace to look ashamed of himself. "No, ma'am, you're in the clear. Not a thing to worry about. The person I'm interested in is a woman who was on the bus when you left Copenhagen. She was wearing a funny hat—"

"Oh. Madame Orkin."

"No, her name is . . ." Christian paused. "Yes, I guess I mean Madame Orkin."

"But you do not suspect her of wrongdoing? Such a kind lady, so thoughtful and pleasant. Speak to her, she will tell you."

"She isn't back yet."

This news disturbed the guide much more than the possibility of being arrested for dealing in drugs.

"Not back! But she must be; we are already behind schedule, we cannot wait. Oh, what shall I do? Wait, I will look. She must be on the bus."

Elizabeth sidled up to Christian. "A tip from a snitch?"

"That is the jargon, I believe." He looked loftily at her down the full length of his nose.

"You are showing signs of a severe personality disturbance," Elizabeth said earnestly. "Quick now—what's your name? Who are you?'

"Don't be absurd. This is no time for facetiousness."

The guide returned. Her frown had intensified and her smile had quite vanished. "Everyone is here but Madame Orkin. I must go back and look for her. Perhaps she was injured. Oh, dear, this is terrible." She began to wring her hands.

At this tense moment deliverance arrived in a most unlikely form—that of a towheaded boy on a bicycle. He looked thoughtfully at the bus and at the unhappy guide; scratched his head; scratched his chin; then produced, from the pocket of his jacket, a letter which he handed to the guide, with a brief explanation in Danish.

The woman's face cleared as if by magic. She opened the letter and turned a beaming smile on Christian.

"It is all right. It is well. See how thoughtful is Madame Orkin; she writes to tell me she had decided to stay in Roskilde tonight. She absolves me of all blame and thanks me. And even . . ." A heavenly glow illumined her face as she took a small wad of Danish banknotes from the envelope. "And even she pays for the luncheon, which she will not eat. It was ordered in advance, you see; she knows that, she thinks of everything. What a good, kind woman is Madame Orkin! She cannot be your drug person, sir."

Quite rejuvenated, she bounded up the stairs onto the bus. Christian pounced on the messenger, who had watched the performance with the tolerant contempt felt by the young for the foibles of the middle-aged. "Where did you get that letter?" he shouted.

"You'll scare the poor child to death," Elizabeth exclaimed.

The boy did not appear at all alarmed. Like most Danes he understood English quite well. "You search for drugs?" he inquired interestedly. "You are a policeman, sir?"

"Er... well... a kind of policeman. You can be of great help."

"But she did not say you were a policeman."

"She? Who?"

"The lady who gave me the letter, and twenty kroner to deliver it to the guide of the large red bus." He glanced calmly at the vehicle, which was making angry noises. "The bus wishes to depart, sir. Shall we move out of its way?"

They did so. The bus departed. Elizabeth hoped the guide enjoyed her lunch. Maybe she would eat two—hers and Margaret's. After all, it had been ordered in advance.

"I'll give you another twenty kroner if you tell me where you saw the lady and what she said," Christian offered, waving the money under the boy's nose.

"You will? That is very generous, sir; for I would have told you anyway, since you are a policeman. It is proper to help the police."

"Quite right," Christian said. "Where—"

"But," the boy continued serenely, "I must deliver this other letter. I do not know who should have it. The lady said the gentleman would be standing near the bus. She said he would be tall and fair, with a great frown on his face. That sounds like you, sir. But would she not have told me that you are a policeman?"

"She just forgot to mention it." Christian snatched the letter and ripped it open.

"I must be sure," the boy insisted. "She was a generous lady, and I do not want to cheat her."

"It's all right," Elizabeth said. She indicated Christian. "Look at that frown. Nobody else frowns like that. Where did you see the lady?"

"At the foot of the hill that goes to the Domkirke." The boy glanced at his watch and added, devastatingly, "It was more than fifteen minutes ago, miss. Can I tell you anything else?"

"No, thank you." Elizabeth twitched the money from Christian's hand and gave it to the boy. "You have done well, young man. *Tak*."

The parking lot was emptying rapidly. Elizabeth took Christian by the arm. He appeared to be rooted to the spot.

"You've done very well up till now," she said kindly. "Don't relapse. Come to the car and sit down. You'll feel better in a minute."

Christian got behind the wheel. "Would you care to see this note?" he inquired distantly.

"Yes, I would. Why do you let her get to you?"

"It's the way she anticipates my every move. And that was a damned insulting description!"

"What, the frowning part? You should see your face right now." Elizabeth took the note.

The writing straggled even more than the famous carousel letter. Elizabeth wondered what Margaret had been doing when she wrote it; swinging across the apse of the Cathedral on a rope?

It began abruptly, without salutation. "This is turning out to be more complicated than I expected. Christian, you must leave Denmark immediately. I don't care where you go, just go, and stand not upon the order.... " The quotation ran out into unintelligibility; Margaret apparently assumed that her point had been made. She resumed, "I cannot tell you what this is all about just yet. Your total ignorance [the phrase was underlined, or perhaps crossed out—the line wove a drunken path partly across the words] of what is going on is your best guarantee of safety. For once in your life do as I ask. Get out of the country. Love, Margaret. P.S. Do not under any circumstances go to the police."

Another inebriated line wavered through the final sentence.

"Cheery, encouraging little epistle, isn't it?" Christian remarked.

"It's straightforward, anyhow. She wants you to clear out."

"Yes, I would say she had made that plain. You should see your face," Christian added maliciously. "Why the scowl?"

"She didn't say anything about me."

"I noticed that. Feelings hurt?"

"Of course not," Elizabeth said in a hurt voice. "Why should she care what happens to me?"

"She would care. She's usually passionately concerned about everybody, even total strangers."

"Then why didn't she even mention me?"

"I refuse to conjecture. We've done too much of that already."

"Are you going to leave?"

"Certainly not." Christian turned on the engine. "How would you like to see a quaint village, or perhaps a thatched cottage?" he inquired kindly.

"Are you kidding? From now on we stick to main roads, and avoid lonely spots and dark alleys."

"I just thought you might like to do a little sightseeing."

"Forget it."

Christian didn't pursue the subject, but as they drove out of the parking lot Elizabeth thought she understood why he had raised it. He wouldn't leave the country, but he intended to see that she did so. The suggestion of sightseeing had been an attempt to appease her frustrated tourist instincts before he evicted her.

They drove around Roskilde for a while, peering out the windows. Elizabeth dutifully peered, but was forced to raise the obvious objection.

"We'd never recognize her even if she's still here. She'll be disguised as a nun, or a Masai warrior, or a Highlander in a kilt."

They stopped for lunch at an inn outside the city.

"I'm glad to see that my near brush with death has not affected your appetite," Christian remarked, when Elizabeth returned from the buffet with a heaped plate.

"I figure I'm going to need my strength. Mmmm—this is marvelous. What is it?"

"Herring, probably," Christian said, eyeing the object on Elizabeth's fork with disfavor. "They try to disguise it in various ways, but it's usually herring."

"I love it. I am going to need my strength," she repeated, "to fight you when you try to shove me onto an airplane."

After a moment Christian said, "I won't ask how you knew that was what I had in mind."

"It's only too obvious." Elizabeth impaled another chunk of herring. "You were being so macho back there at the Cathedral, flexing your muscles and shrugging your shoulders at bullets; the next step is to get the helpless little woman out of the path of peril."

"Elizabeth Jones."

Elizabeth looked up, startled by his tone. He was studying her with a bewildered look. "Two days ago I didn't know you from Adam," he said. "And here you are playing Girl Friday.... All right, I take it back—playing faithful sidekick or Watson, or whatever equal and nonsexist role you like. That was fine so long as our activities were confined to chasing Margaret around Copenhagen and responding to imbecile demands for objects we didn't want anyway. But there is no reason on God's earth why you should stick around after the bullets start flying."

"I don't blame your mother for running away from you," Elizabeth snapped. "She told me you were bossy; well, you're not going to boss me. You can't make me leave if I don't want to."

"Any woman in her right mind—if there is such a person—would want to. She'd be screaming to get out of this mess. Why are you so determined to risk your neck? Bullets don't always hit the target they're aimed at, you know."

Somewhere in the back of her mind was an answer to that question, but Elizabeth wasn't ready to admit it even to herself. She sought refuge in frivolity.

"Frenchton and Monk would fire me if I let their favorite author get lost. I've made up my mind. I don't intend to discuss it any further."

She stood up. "Where are you going?" Christian asked.

"For more herring."

They went on arguing all the way back to Copenhagen, not only about whether or not Elizabeth should leave the country, but about what their next move should be.

"The only sensible thing is to stick around the hotel," Christian said finally. "She knows how to reach us—me—and I don't know how to reach her. When she sees we—I mean, I am not going to make plane reservations, maybe she'll get in touch with us—me, I meant to say."

It sounded, Elizabeth thought, as if she were in for a long, boring evening.

But no sooner had they entered the hotel than Marie ran to meet them. Her sleek gray hair was disheveled, and her smiling calm had given way to excitement.

"Thank heaven you are here! We have looked all over the city for you; Roger, poor Roger—"

"Now, Marie, be calm." Her husband appeared in the door of the office. He was as impeccably turned out as ever, but his extremely high forehead was embellished by a white bandage.

"Good Lord, Roger," Christian exclaimed.

"It is nothing," Roger said quickly. "I surprised a thief in Margaret's room, that is all. Our security system is intentionally unobtrusive; I suppose he did not observe the wire when he forced the door. I went up at once. He was very quick; or perhaps I am just getting old!"

"Nonsense." His wife turned to him with fond indignation. "You could have been killed, my dear."

"I can't tell you how sorry I am," Christian said.

"It is my duty, and my pleasure. But I am glad you are here. You will please look to see if anything was stolen."

"I will, of course, but that doesn't matter. Margaret would rather lose everything she owns than see you injured, Roger. Why don't you lie down? I'll check, and let you know."

"No, no, I am not hurt, it is only a bump. I wish to make sure all is well with Margaret. Do you know when she will be returning?"

"Uh—no. Not exactly. Well, let's go up, then."

Roger had interrupted the thief before he really got to work. A single bureau drawer stood ajar. There was no other sign of disturbance.

"I'm sure it's all right," Christian said.

"Please do me the favor to see if any cash, traveler's checks, or jewelry is missing," Roger insisted.

"She kept cash and traveler's checks in her handbag," Christian said. "And she never carries much jewelry."

Roger continued to urge; Christian continued to reassure him. Convinced at last, the hotel manager's face brightened and he let out a sigh of relief. "Excellent. We are very fortunate. I will so inform the police."

"The police have been here?"

"I had to make a report. I promised to inform them if anything was missing." Seeing Christian's frown, he added reassuringly, "I doubt they will wish to interview you, since you have lost nothing and did not see the thief."

"That's right, you saw him. What did he look like?"

"I did not get a good look. He was very quick to hit me on the head." Roger touched his bandage gingerly. "He was not young and not old; only a few lines around his eyes. They were dark, as was his hair, except for gray streaks at each temple. . . . What, do you know him?"

"No. No, I was just surprised . . . that he wasn't some kid, some young punk."

It was not a very convincing explanation for his stifled exclamation and start of surprise, but Roger seemed to accept it. After a further exchange of compliments the manager took his leave, and Christian and Elizabeth spoke at once.

"It was him!"

"Mr. Schmidt!"

"But what was he looking for?" Elizabeth asked.

"If we knew that, we'd have the answers to a lot of other questions." Christian peered into the open drawer.

"That's underwear," Elizabeth said. "I put it away myself. Schmidt didn't strike me as the type that steals women's lingerie."

"I am inclined to agree. Whatever he was after, we can assume he didn't have time to find it. Let's have a look—especially at Margaret's notes and papers."

The search took over an hour. Since they had no idea what they were looking for, they had to read every note and inspect every scrap of paper. The only thing that emerged from their investigation was that Margaret did have a great deal of material about Queen Margaret the First of Denmark.

"It appears that you were wrong about the biography," Elizabeth said, thumbing through a Xeroxed copy of a Danish biography of the lady in question. "She has definitely started her research."

The telephone rang just then and they both jumped for it. But it was only Roger inquiring whether they planned to dine in that evening.

"The kitchen is back to normal, thank heaven. I cannot imagine what illness struck us; we have found nothing to account for it. So if you would care to order . . ."

"Yes, fine, anything," Christian said. He added, politely, "I hope all the sufferers are healthy again."

"Yes, I thank you for asking; all but Froken Blixen, our receptionist and telephone operator. She has had a relapse, nothing serious, but she will not be able to return to work for a while. The new girl is not as efficient as I would like, but she will do until then. Would you like, perhaps, a blanquette of veal with new peas and potatoes? And for the wine . . . "

The prospect of drinking something other than beer revived Christian's interest. While he and Roger engaged in an animated discussion about vintages, Elizabeth began another search of Margaret's papers. She had the feeling she had missed something, but could not think what it could be.

She was still reading when the food was delivered, and even the excellent rosé did not distract her until Christian spoke.

"What are you looking for?"

"I wish I knew. All this material seems to bear on Queen Margaret; it's precisely the sort of thing I would expect to find if she were getting ready to write a biography. At least I think it is; I can't read Danish. What about this?"

She handed Christian a newspaper clipping. He shook his head over it. "As you have remarked, my own Danish isn't that fluent. This seems to be a story about damage to the abbey church at Sorø, wherever that is. An ancient Cistercian abbey with some royal tombs. I can't make out the rest."

"I thought all the Danish kings were buried at Roskilde," Elizabeth said.

"I thought so, too. But," Christian added, "I don't really care."

Among the items in the folders was the photograph of Queen Margaret's cloth-of-gold robe. "How I'd love to see it," Elizabeth murmured. "Where is Uppsala?"

"Sweden. But the thing isn't much to look at. I don't know why women are so fascinated by clothes. Especially worn out, moldy old clothes."

"Men have no imagination." Elizabeth spoke absently. She was thinking about something else—or rather, trying to catch an elusive idea that kept slipping through her mental grasp. "Christian?"

"I'm still here."

"About the bathrobe . . . You don't suppose they meant Queen Margaret's bathrobe?"

Christian's fork stopped an inch from his mouth. He considered the suggestion.

"There are a number of Margarets in this affair," he conceded. "You are, I presume, aware of the fact that the present ruler of Denmark is Margaret the Second."

"That's right! That makes even better sense. A royal bathrobe would be worth—"

"Oh, for God's sake, Elizabeth, get a grip on yourself. You don't suppose the queen trails around her bedroom in ermine and gowns clanking with jewels? I am not familiar with the personal wardrobes of royalty, but I'd lay odds that even reigning monarchs wear comfortable woolly robes. Castles are drafty places."

"It was just a thought."

"And a damned stupid one. Eat your dinner."

It turned out to be a very dull evening, just as Elizabeth had expected. Christian pretended to read, but he turned an average of one page every five minutes. Elizabeth tried to absorb herself in Margaret's notes, but was unable to concentrate. Her eyes kept wandering to the telephone, willing it to ring. Finally she gave up. When she switched on the television set Christian said, "Everything will be in Danish, you know."

"I don't care. I just want to sit and stare stupidly at something that moves."

She had no trouble selecting a channel. There was only one. But to her pleased surprise the sounds that came from the speaker were in English.

"It's a movie," she exclaimed. "With Danish subtitles."

"Must be as old as the hills," Christian said. "It's in black and white."

"Shush. I have to concentrate."

She had missed the first part of the film, but it did not take long to figure out the plot; the film techniques of the nineteen forties were straightforward and simple, and this film had no pretensions to artistic subtlety. It was a thriller, all about Nazis and a pair of brave young Americans trying to

rescue an imprisoned scientist. Elizabeth did not recognize
any of the actors. The chief Nazi villain looked vaguely
familiar, and for some time she puzzled over where she had
seen him before. Then the answer came: Mr. Schmidt. It
wasn't Schmidt, of course, but the faces had the same char-
acteristics—the predatory front teeth, the eyes just a little too
close together.

The young couple, Bob and Mary, were winsome and
young and witty. It was obvious by the middle of the film
that they had fallen in love, but for some reason neither of
them would admit it; they kept bickering and exchanging
insults and pretending to be indifferent. At one point they
had to share a hotel room, in order to maintain their cover as
husband and wife. The convolutions this situation entailed
would have dated the film to a bygone era even if the costumes and techniques had not. Elizabeth smiled patronizingly as the blushing heroine lay with the covers pulled up to
her nose, rolling her eyes at the hero, who was uncomfort-
ably ensconced in a chair.

Christian affected great disdain for this unintellectual
entertainment, but as the film went on he kept casting
glances at the screen, and before long he was watching as
intently as Elizabeth. The gallant young pair got the dodder-
ing old scientist away, but were themselves captured, right
on the Swiss frontier, by the sneering Nazi officer, who carried them off in triumph to his lair in an elegant mountain
chateau.

It was the great scene for the actor who played the Nazi,
and he made the most of it, leering till his cheeks must have
ached. Naturally the adventurers steadfastly refused to give
away the whereabouts of the scientist. Cracking his whip
against his polished boots, the officer advanced on the
shrinking heroine.

"So, *Fräulein*, you will not speak, *ja*? But I think you will
speak, *ja, ja*. Tell me what I wish to know, or that beautiful
face will not be so beautiful in future, *ja?*"

He raised his whip. The girl shrieked. Disdaining the weapons trained on him, the hero leaped at the Nazi and hit him on the jaw.

He was immediately knocked down by one of the guards. The girl rushed to his side.

"Bob," she sobbed, raising his unconscious head into her arms. "Oh, Bob, darling!"

"Oh, Christ," said Christian, disgustedly.

"Shush," said Elizabeth.

For reasons known only to the writer of the script—and perhaps not even to him—the villain, upon recovering, threw the young couple into the cellar instead of carrying on with his attempt to make them talk. The hero used his pocket knife—which the Nazis had apparently overlooked when they searched him—to pry out one of the bars in the window. As he and the heroine departed he lit the fuse on a keg of dynamite which had been conveniently left in the cellar, and the escape of the lovers was marked by a magnificent explosion that annihilated the sneering officer, the guards, and the chateau.

"What a piece of trash," Christian said, as the credits rolled across the screen.

"Wasn't it, though," said Elizabeth. She laughed. "It's amazing how filmmaking has advanced since then."

"I'm not talking about film technique; I don't see many movies, I have better things to do with my time. But you would think the idiots could at least write a coherent story. The relationship between those two was so unrealistic—"

"Sexual mores were different then."

"They weren't different, they were just more hypocritical. The dumbest thing of all was at the end, when the villain was threatening the girl and that klutz jumped him. Why would he do a stupid thing like that?"

"He loved her," Elizabeth said, very gently.

"Yes, fine, but what was the point? He couldn't do her any good by getting himself killed or knocked unconscious. If he had been so smart as he was supposed to be—"

"I'm going to bed," Elizabeth said. "Good night."

"What's the matter?"

"Nothing."

She had not intended to slam the door; it more or less slammed itself. I don't know what's bugging me, Elizabeth thought, brushing her teeth so violently that toothpaste flew all over the bathroom. He's right. It was a dumb, stupid movie.

✂ 7 ✂

BY MIDMORNING there had been no word from Margaret or anyone else, and Christian had given up all pretense at calm reason. After searching Margaret's belongings again, and leaving them in such a mess that it took Elizabeth half an hour to straighten them out, he flung himself at the telephone and began calling people. This proved to be worse than useless. Margaret's friends were thrilled to hear that she was in Denmark, and they plied Christian with invitations he was unable to accept and questions he was unable to answer. Still, he pressed doggedly on. As he prepared to dial for the sixth time, Elizabeth said, "How can she call us if you're on the phone all the time?"

"Hmph." Christian replaced the receiver. "I didn't really expect her to telephone. She hasn't since that first call."

"Don't you find that rather curious?"

"What do you mean?"

"Well, I think that when she first walked out of here she didn't expect to be gone long—maybe not even a whole day. In the note she wrote yesterday she admitted her business was more complicated than she had expected. She took the trouble to communicate with you, and warn you. Maybe your presence or your snooping is endangering her project, or maybe it's endangering you personally. In view of the fact that someone took a shot at you yesterday I'm inclined to think the second alternative is the more plausible. So why hasn't she called to reinforce her warning? Why does she write frantic notes instead of picking up the phone? She could call from a public telephone without giving away her whereabouts."

Christian followed this somewhat incoherent reasoning with a wrinkled brow. "She has never bothered to call before when she was off on some insane escapade."

"But they were all harmless escapades—harmless to you, at any rate."

"I think I see what you're getting at. But all you've done is raise another question we can't answer."

"I know. But I have a feeling there's a pattern in this somewhere, if we could only put it together."

Christian picked up the jacket he had worn the day before. The holes in the sleeve seemed to hold a morbid fascination for him. He put his finger through one of them and wriggled it.

"Don't do that," Elizabeth snapped.

"Why not?" But he tossed the jacket onto a chair. "Sitting around here is driving me demented," he growled. "I've got to do something."

"There's one obvious thing to do."

"All sorts of things seem obvious to you. What is it this time?"

"Go to the police, of course." He stared at her, his lip out-thrust and mutinous. Elizabeth went on urgently, "You have enough evidence now to force Mr. Grundtvig to take you seriously. The bullet holes in your jacket, the break-in here . . ."

"I'm not going to go crawling to that opinionated old jack-ass."

"Just because he kept calling you 'young Christian.' "

"Damn it, he was patronizing me. I'm thirty-two years old—"

"Are you really? I'd have said you were older."

"Oh?" Christian looked pleased.

"He's the logical person to talk to," Elizabeth insisted.

"She told me not to go to the police."

"Everybody told us not to go to the police. So what? Grundtvig is highly placed, and he is an old buddy of Margaret's; he can function discreetly, without danger of publicity to her." Christian did not reply, and she added angrily, "I can't understand why you resist the idea. You're the type I would expect to go running to the authorities at the first sign of trouble."

This comment was meant as an insult and was taken as such. Christian's cheeks reddened. "Listen, I never claimed to be, or wanted to be, one of those fool adventurers you seem to admire. A sane, law-abiding person would naturally seek police assistance in case of trouble."

"Then why aren't you doing it?"

Having painted himself into a corner, logically speaking, Christian jumped up and began pacing, his back to her. "I don't have to explain my motives to you," he said over his shoulder. "I'll give her another twenty-four hours. If we haven't heard anything by then, I'll talk to Grundtvig."

Elizabeth knew that tone. The more she argued, the more stubborn he would get. "Oh, all right," she said.

"What do you mean, all right?" He spun around. "You have nothing to say about it. You're out of this. I'd have called and made a plane reservation for you before this if I hadn't been afraid Margaret would find out about it and think I was obeying her orders."

"Oh, let's not argue about that," Elizabeth said wearily. "It's a waste of time and energy. You think of her as omniscient, don't you? The last time we saw her she was miles from here, heading God knows where; she can't possibly know what you are doing every minute of the day."

"You haven't thought that one out, have you?" The idea that he was ahead of her in one area at least calmed Christian's temper. His face relaxed into an expression that was less forbidding, if not actually pleasant. "Why do you think I've been calling her friends? She has to be staying somewhere; she couldn't register at a hotel without showing her passport, and she would be reluctant to do that. Her name is too well known. She would avoid cashing traveler's checks for the same reason. Where is she getting money? And—think this one over—how did she know we were going to Tivoli the other night? Did you think it was pure coincidence that she was on the carousel at the precise time we were supposed to deliver the suitcase?"

"Naturally I wondered about that," Elizabeth said stoutly. "Maybe she was following us."

"Disguised as a skinhead on a motorcycle?" Christian thought that one over; his sneer faded. "Well, maybe . . . Damn it, no, she can't be everywhere. She has friends all over the place, and most of them would cheerfully spy for her if she asked them to, without asking for explanations. I'm not sure Roger and Marie aren't in touch with her."

"Surely not. They know how worried you are."

"Margaret hypnotizes people. She's as bad as Hitler."

Elizabeth did not feel this outrageous comment deserved a reply.

Christian returned to the telephone and his address book.

"Now who are you calling?"

"Someone I should have contacted before this. He's the director of the National Museum, and an old boyfriend of Margaret's."

For want of anything better to do, Elizabeth listened while he made the call and found that she was able to follow the action fairly well, thanks to the fact that the conversation consisted mostly of names. From the museum switchboard Christian was passed to a secretary, who informed him that the director was busy. Could she take a message? Christian mentioned his name, then listened, said, *"Ja, god; tak,"* and hung up.

"He'll see us this afternoon," he announced. "He was on his way to a meeting."

"You want to go to the museum? Why can't he call you back?"

"I'd just as soon get out of here for a while. I'm starting to suffer from claustrophobia."

"I think you ought to stay inside."

"Nobody is going to shoot me in broad daylight on the streets of Copenhagen," Christian said firmly.

"They took a shot at you in broad daylight in Roskilde Cathedral. You can't get much more public than that."

"So we'll drive." He added nastily, "If you're afraid of being caught in the line of fire you can stay here."

"I wouldn't dream of it. Maybe I'll have a chance to see some of the museum before they shoot you."

After an excellent lunch, to which neither of them did justice, Christian called the desk and asked that the car be brought around. It was waiting at the curb when they came out of the hotel, and Roger himself was at the wheel. He handed over the keys. "Off to do a little sightseeing?" he inquired genially.

His bandage had been replaced by a square of white gauze. "That's encouraging," Elizabeth said. "I hope it means you are feeling better."

"Oh, yes, certainly; I told you it was nothing. Where are you going this afternoon?"

"Sightseeing." Elizabeth didn't share Christian's suspicions of the friendly manager, but his interest in their plans made her cautious about giving away more information than was necessary.

"Enjoy yourselves." He turned to Christian, who had gone to the front of the car and lifted the hood. "Is something the matter, Christian?"

"I thought I heard a *ping* yesterday." Christian peered into the engine.

"It sounded fine when I drove it," Roger said. "Shall I send for a mechanic?"

"No, I guess it's okay." Christian lowered the hood. "Thanks, Roger."

As they pulled away from the curb, Elizabeth said, "What were you looking for? A bomb?"

"Just a precaution."

"Would you know a bomb if you saw one?"

Christian did not reply.

Elizabeth assumed they would be unable to find a parking place near the museum, and she was dreading the walk, however short; but Christian's concern for his skin inspired him to new heights of inventiveness. He drove straight into the lot reserved for museum officials, told the attendant he was the director's son-in-law, and tipped him profusely.

"Smart," Elizabeth admitted, as they entered the central courtyard. "Illegal, but smart."

"Why don't you look at the exhibits while I—"

"Why don't you shut up?"

The museum had been high on Elizabeth's list of "Things to See in Copenhagen." Costumes, folk art, golden treasures from Iron Age tombs, Viking weapons and jewelry... She did not even glance into the exhibition hall before they climbed the staircase toward the director's offices. She had no intention of admitting it to Christian, but she was determined to stick to him like a burr. No doubt it was naive to think she could protect him; a skilled marksman could pick him off before she realized that a gun was trained on him. But the marksman of the Cathedral had missed, and in certain situations the presence of a second person, constantly on the alert, might mean the difference between life and death.

Frederick Leinsdorf was the most beautiful old man she had ever seen. Gleaming silver hair framed a face of such delicate grace that it might have been carved from ivory by a medieval master. The hand he extended in greeting was as finely shaped as his features, with long, sensitive fingers. Even the outstanding veins and tendons of old age seemed part of a classic structure of design.

She had hoped that Leinsdorf's eminent position and look of quiet integrity might move Christian to be more candid about the situation than he had been with others; but Christian was still playing it cool.

"Margaret is off on another of her wild adventures," he said casually. "You are one of her oldest friends, so you know how she is; but it's been several days now, and I'm a little concerned. I thought perhaps you had heard from her."

"No, I have not." Leinsdorf folded his hands and looked pensive. Then his face broke into a broad, amused smile. "Of course I might be lying."

"Are you?" Christian asked bluntly.

"No." Leinsdorf's smile faded. "I knew Margaret was in Denmark. I had a telephone call from a man named Grundtvig, who is—"

"I know who he is," Christian interrupted. "Are you a friend of his?"

"Not a personal friend, no. I know of him, naturally. He is prominent in his own field. Like you, he asked if I had heard from Margaret."

So Grundtvig had taken their inquiries more seriously than he had pretended, and had begun to make inquiries of his own. Elizabeth found this encouraging; Christian's frown indicated that he was not pleased.

"Is there any reason why he would call you in particular?" he asked suspiciously.

"He may have called others; I did not inquire." Leinsdorf looked at Christian quizzically. "May I ask if there is any reason why you called on me—in particular?"

Christian hesitated. "This is going to sound fantastic."

"Naturally, if Margaret is involved in it." Leinsdorf's attractive smile warmed his austere face. "Go on."

"I have a suspicion that Margaret's current activities may involve Queen Margaret. The medieval one, not the present queen."

Leinsdorf's expression did not change, but his long, graceful hands tightened till the tendons stood out like cords. "In what way?" he asked quietly.

"I wish I knew. Margaret was thinking of writing a biography of the queen—or so she said. The last few days . . .Well, I'd rather not go into detail, but Queen Margaret's name keeps cropping up, as it were. You're a historian and a medievalist. I thought maybe . . ."

He gestured helplessly. Leinsdorf lowered his eyes and appeared to be intent on a pile of papers on the desk. Elizabeth had the feeling that he was not so much avoiding their gaze as trying to veil his own.

"If you could be more specific, perhaps I could help you," he said finally.

"I can't. That's all I know."

"Margaret did not confide in you?"

"No." Christian hated to admit it. His voice was sour. "The question is, did she confide in you?"

"No." The reply was prompt, and apparently sincere. Leinsdorf seemed to come to a decision. "I can give you no information, Christian. But I will see what I can find out, and I promise that if I learn anything you ought to know, I will inform you at once. Where are you staying?"

His tone made it clear that the interview was over. Christian gave him the address of the hotel, and after the usual compliments and thanks, they took their leave.

Once outside the office, Christian's smile vanished. He hit his fist against the wall. "What a crafty liar that man is! Did you notice how carefully he phrased his statements? If he learns anything I ought to know. . . And he'll be the one who decides whether I ought to know it."

"He said flat out that he hadn't heard from Margaret."

"He also said he could be lying."

"I don't believe he was. As you said, he was careful about committing himself. He didn't say he had no information, he said he was unable to give it to you. He knows something we don't know; but I believe he was telling the truth when he denied having heard from Margaret."

"We didn't get much out of that interview, did we?" Christian took her arm as they started down the stairs.

"One thing. Queen Margaret is involved, somehow. The mention of her name really jolted him."

"That only makes matters worse," Christian grumbled. "I had hoped we could eliminate Queen Margaret; she's the chief source of confusion in this damned affair."

"No, she's not."

"Then what is?"

"The bathrobe."

"What bathrobe? Oh . . ."

"You mean *whose* bathrobe. And *why* the bathrobe."

"You would have to bring that up. Forget the damned bathrobe. I have."

"I wish I could. It keeps nibbling away at the base of my subconscious mind."

"Forget it," Christian repeated, with such vehemence that Elizabeth suspected the bathrobe was bugging him as much as it nagged at her.

"Let's call Grundtvig. Please, Christian. You see, he did take you seriously. He's looking for Margaret too. Maybe he's found out something."

"Then why hasn't he condescended to inform me? No. I said tomorrow morning, and I meant tomorrow morning." Christian stopped. "I wonder . . . Does the museum have a medieval section?"

Conflicting emotions warred in Elizabeth's breast. "I don't think we should linger here. There are too many people around."

"We can't afford to overlook a possible clue. I'll bet you have that handy little guidebook with you."

If he had shouted or snapped at her she might have persisted. His cool reasonableness, and his attractive and infrequent smile, had a peculiarly weakening effect on her. Besides, what he had suggested made sense. Leinsdorf's reaction to the mention of Queen Margaret lent credence to the idea that the lady, if not her bathrobe, was an integral part of the affair. It was a far-out chance that the museum might contain any pertinent material, but they were in no position to neglect any possibility.

Conquering her vague forebodings of danger, she reached in her purse and produced the guidebook. "They do have some objects from Margaret's time. 'Historical Period; 1000 to 1750 A.D. Rooms 23 to 29.' That's on the first floor—second floor to us."

When they reached the second-floor landing, a closed door and a printed sign barred entrance. " 'Closed for rebuilding,' " Christian read. "Damn."

"Maybe it's just as well." Elizabeth glanced uneasily over her shoulder. In contrast to the crowded halls below, this part of the museum seemed deserted. Either it was not as popular as Viking treasures, or else potential seekers of wisdom possessed a more up-to-date guidebook.

An unpopulated museum can seem emptier and more uncanny than any other building. The vast, high-ceilinged rooms hum with sounds just beyond the range of hearing— probably the products of air conditioning and security systems, but oddly suggestive of surreptitious movements within the cases, as though invisible hands were fumbling to repossess tools and weapons and ornaments.

"Come on," Elizabeth said nervously.

"Wait a minute. It says some articles are on special exhibit in rooms 34 and 35. We'll have to go around the other way."

In so doing they followed the exhibits in reverse order of time—from furniture of the early baroque to rooms furnished in the style of 1625, to Lutheran church regalia of a century before that. The rooms were not entirely empty of human life. A bored elderly guard watched them suspiciously as they passed a cabinet containing silver plate, and a young woman, presumably an art-history student, was sketching a carved altarpiece. Their presence did nothing to relieve the general atmosphere of echoing emptiness, and twice, when they paused for a moment, Elizabeth thought she heard footsteps behind them—soft, sly steps that paused just outside the door of the room in which they were. Well, and why not? she reassured herself. There are other people interested in medieval Denmark.

Still, she was relieved when they had left the later centuries behind and saw objects dating to the fifteenth. They moved slowly here, reading every label, but it soon became depressingly apparent that there was nothing in the exhibit pertaining to Margaret the First. The majority of the exhibits were religious in nature—chalices and copes and chasubles, altarpieces and sculptures of saints. In the final room a temporary door blocked further progress.

"I guess that's all," Christian said. "It was a forlorn hope at best. We'll have to go back the way we came in."

He strode toward the door. Elizabeth was right on his heels. Those soft, surreptitious footsteps still worried her. She was beside him when they passed into the next room, but he was the one who saw the flicker of movement as a figure darted into concealment behind a painted communion table.

"Hey, you," Christian shouted. He moved so quickly that the hand Elizabeth flung out, in a vain attempt to stop him, missed its grasp by a good six inches.

Realizing he had been seen, the man came out of hiding. Elizabeth let out a shriek that shattered the sacred silence and made the glass in the cases rattle. It was rather like screaming in church, but she didn't care; the more people who heard her, the better, as far as she was concerned. For the figure was one she had seen before—the meager, shabby man who had dropped his trunk on Margaret's secretary.

The room was one of the larger exhibition halls, a good sixty feet long, but Christian was covering the distance in great uninhibited bounds. The shabby little man cast a quick measuring look at the exit and another at Christian, closing in on him, and decided against flight. His hand moved toward his pocket. As Christian reached out for him he ducked back behind the communion table. Following, Christian slipped and lost his balance. He grabbed the edge of the table and managed to remain upright, until the little man, reappearing, hit him smartly over the head with a short blunt instrument. Christian fell down, Elizabeth ran toward him, and the little man departed at a sedate trot.

By the time Elizabeth reached him Christian was sitting up, rubbing his head. With her aid, and that of the communion table, he got to his feet, but he was still leaning dizzily on the table when the guard came puffing in. Instead of offering sympathy or assistance, the guard let out an indignant cry and burst into passionate speech. From his gestures Elizabeth gathered that he was scolding Christian for touching one of the antiques.

Christian had to calm not only the guard but an indignant Elizabeth. As he dragged her bodily from the scene, he hissed, "For God's sake, he was only doing his job! He didn't know I had been hit on the head, he didn't know what the hell you were bellowing about, and even if he had, he's too old and fat and underpaid to risk his neck chasing muggers."

"Well . . .That's true. I wasn't really mad at *him*."

"I assume you are not unreasonable enough to be mad at *me*. It wasn't *my* fault. *I* didn't ask to be hit on the head."

"You might as well have."

"Thanks for the sympathy! Whatever happened to the ministering-angel routine?"

"Are you hurt?" Elizabeth inquired, somewhat belatedly.

"No."

"You aren't going to get any sympathy playing stoic." But her voice was unsteady, and when Christian glanced down at her he saw something in her face that improved his temper.

"I'm fine. He didn't hit hard. Either he missed, being in something of a hurry, or . . . "

"Or what?"

"Or he didn't intend to hit hard."

Elizabeth had no intention of taking his word for it. His nonchalance about danger worried her almost as much as did her suspicion that deep down underneath he was beginning to enjoy the excitement. There was more of his mother in him than any of them, including Christian, had realized.

As soon as they got in the car she put her hands on his head and inspected his skull for damage. He gave her a startled look, but submitted without comment; and she was soon able to satisfy herself that he had not been playing hero. The rising bump was trivial and the skin had not been broken.

"It doesn't make sense," she said, as they drove through the thickening traffic of late afternoon. "Yesterday they tried to shoot you. Today—he could have picked you off a dozen times, do you realize that?"

"He didn't have a gun." Christian slammed on the brakes and swore as a Saab cut in front of him. "At least, the thing he hit me with wasn't a gun. It is confusing. Maybe there are two gangs after us."

Elizabeth did not find this idea comforting. "I don't suppose this little encounter has convinced you that we ought to go to the police?"

"You are correct. It hasn't."

"You're impossible," Elizabeth said angrily. "Once you make up your mind, you never change it."

But she was mistaken. He changed his mind an hour or so later, when they got the package containing the severed human finger.

8

AFTER Elizabeth was through being sick, she returned to the sitting room. The box, a small cardboard container some six inches square, rested on the coffee table. Knees on his elbows, face faintly green, Christian was staring at it.

Elizabeth carefully selected a chair far enough from the table so that she was unable to see into the depths of the box. She remembered, only too well, what the grisly object was like. Nestled cozily in a bed of cotton wool, it had been covered by another layer of the same material. When Christian lifted this off, Elizabeth's eyes had refused to believe what they saw. Pallidly, loathsomely white and bloodless, the object had resembled a marble or plaster imitation of the real thing, carved with a consummate skill that reproduced every line, every hair, every pore.

She had made it to the bathroom just in time. Now, shaken and ashamed of her weakness, she said resolutely, "Is it Margaret's?"

"It could be. Would you recognize an isolated finger if you saw it separated from its owner?"

His tone contrasted painfully with the calm precision of his words. "My dear," she began.

Christian appeared not to hear the endearment. "It's possible that this is just another trick to alarm us. But I can't take that chance. Naturally, I'll go."

"Go where?"

"There is a note." The greenish tint on Christian's face deepened. "It was under the finger."

He had had to touch it—lift it, perhaps. Unpleasant enough if it had been some anonymous digit, owner unknown. Recalling the countless times he had held his mother's hand, twined his childish fingers around hers. . . . Enough of that, Elizabeth told herself.

"What does the note say?"

"It gives a time and a place. Presumably I'm to be there."

"Where?"

"It says, 'Come alone.' " Christian's lips twisted in a sardonic smile. "Apparently they are getting tired of you hanging around all the time."

"I will be, though."

"You will not." Christian picked up the piece of paper, holding it with his fingertips, almost as fastidiously as he would have held the amputated finger. " 'If you are accompanied, you will not be contacted, and tomorrow you will receive the mate to this.' "

She could put forth no argument to annul the brutality of the threat. Desperation showed her her only weapon.

"If you go without me, I'll call Grundtvig and tell him everything."

His stiff face came to life. "You wouldn't."

"Christian, think! You made fun of the hero of that movie last night because he risked his life uselessly. That's exactly what you are proposing to do. They won't release Margaret—if they have her—in exchange for you. They want something you don't have—you don't even know what it is! You'll only succeed in getting yourself captured or killed, and she'll be in as much trouble as she is already. More; because I suspect she's rather fond of you."

She put every ounce of persuasion she could summon into her voice and her expression, and died a dozen deaths while Christian thought it over.

"I suppose you're right," he said, after an eon.

Elizabeth breathed. "Then . . ." she began.

"Yes, damn it, all right! The time has come to talk to Papa Grundtvig. I may be stubborn, but I'm not stupid."

He reached for the telephone. "Get on the extension in Margaret's room," he said.

Elizabeth was glad he had suggested it. She had every intention of listening anyway, but it was nice to have permission.

By the time she lifted the receiver he had been put through. The click of her entrance into the conversation did not go unnoticed; Grundtvig was trained in such matters.

"There is someone on the line," he said sharply.

"It's just me," Elizabeth said apologetically.

"Miss Jones? How nice to speak to you again."

"Never mind that," Christian said. He had been slow to make up his mind, but once it was made up he did not equivocate. "I must see you right away, Mr. Grundtvig. A number of alarming things have happened, and I have reason to believe Margaret is in serious—"

"Be quiet!" The tone was so sharp that Christian stopped in midsentence. Grundtvig went on, "Don't say any more. Don't come here. I will see you at my home, tonight. Do you have a pencil? I will give you the address."

"Yes, I'm ready. It has to be early, Mr. Grundtvig. There is something I may have to do later."

"Seven o'clock. The address is Horsensgade 37. Do not walk or take a taxi. Drive your own car."

He hung up.

Elizabeth went back to the sitting room. Christian was staring blankly at the telephone. "Well, what do you know abut that?" he muttered.

"He knows something."

"Everybody knows something except us. I'm not sure I like this development."

"I don't like any of it."

"I mean the insistence on secrecy. Maybe Margaret is mixed up in something illegal."

"She wouldn't."

"Ha, ha."

Elizabeth decided to abandon the argument; she had a feeling that her defense of Margaret was the weaker side. "What was that you said about a late date?" she asked accusingly.

"Grundtvig may want me to keep that appointment. Properly protected—"

"He can't protect you from a shot out of the dark."

"Let's wait and see what he says. You were the one who insisted we put the matter into his hands."

Elizabeth bit her lip. She hadn't anticipated this. A police official might well expect Christian to keep the appointment.

"You know," Christian went on, "I don't think this is Margaret's finger."

"No? That's good. Why not?"

"Look at it."

Elizabeth hastily retreated as he lifted the box. "Oh, all right, don't look at it," Christian said. "Did you notice that there's no blood? And unless my sense of smell has gone haywire, I detect a faint but perceptible odor of formaldehyde."

"I'll take your word for it," Elizabeth said, continuing to back away.

"If this thing has been chopped off a living person, it wouldn't be so neat," Christian continued, ignoring her nauseated expression. "In fact, they would want it to look as gruesome as possible, wouldn't they? Clotted with gore—"

"I see what you're driving at. You needn't elaborate."

"I thought you'd be pleased."

"I am. I'm delirious with joy. So you think this object was removed from someone already dead. . . . Christian! It couldn't be hers—the other Margaret's?"

Christian looked startled. Then he laughed. "Hardly. Five hundred and some years dead . . . There wouldn't be anything left but bones. If that." He picked up the box and studied the contents. There was no distress on his face now, only curiosity. "All the same—it looks like a woman's finger."

II

Rewrapped and retied with the original cord, the box was in Christian's pocket when they left the hotel. Grundtvig had not given them directions, and they had decided it would be best not to ask. A city map had provided the necessary information, and Christian appeared to have no doubt about where he was going.

Grundtvig's house was in the northern suburbs of the city. Small and unpretentious, like all the other houses on the block, it appeared to be a product of the state building program. In contrast to the beautifully tended gardens and grass of neighboring houses, Grundtvig's lawn was weedy and neglected

He was at the door before Christian could knock. His round, rosy face bore a look of comical distress.

"My daughter is here," he said, in a hoarse, confidential whisper. "Don't say anything in front of—"

A voice called out from the room beyond the tiny entrance hall. Grundtvig turned. "It is my friends, come to visit," he answered.

A tall, heavy-set woman appeared in the doorway. Blond hair was tucked firmly into a bun at the back of her neck, and her face bore a striking resemblance to her father's, in contour, if not in expression. Her lips were pressed firmly together, her eyes were curious.

"My daughter, Mrs. Brandes," Grundtvig said. "Er—my dear, may I introduce Mr. Umblum and Miss Erglub."

"How do you do." Mrs. Brandes seized first Elizabeth's hand and then Christian's in a manly grip. "You are American?"

"Er—yes," Christian said. "We happened to be passing. . . .That is, we happened to be in Denmark. . . ."

"And you came to call on Papa. That was kind."

"Our pleasure," Christian mumbled.

"Are you perhaps professional associates of—"

"My dear," Grundtvig interrupted. "Did you not say you were meeting Karl? You will be late."

Mrs. Brandes shot out a muscular arm and consulted her wristwatch. "No, I will be precisely on time. I am never late, Papa; you know that. You will forgive me if I run away now. I am sorry I cannot stay."

"Nice to have met you," Christian said.

"And I am pleased to meet you. Papa, you will not forget your medicine? I will call later to make sure you—"

"I promise, I will not forget. Run along now, my dear."

When she had gone Grundtvig shook his head and laughed. Elizabeth thought the laugh sounded a trifle strained.

"Forgive me that I did not give your names. Had she known you were Margaret's son, she would gossip to her husband and everyone else she met."

"She seems devoted to you," Elizabeth said.

"She is, she is." Grundtvig's face took on a look of profound gloom. "She does this often—dropping in, is that the English phrase? It is very nice, I am sure. But come in, come in, we do not have to stand in the hall."

The small living room was stuffed with furniture, photographs, and bric-a-brac. Everything was old-fashioned and a trifle shabby, but impeccably neat. Elizabeth commented on the neatness, thinking to please. Grundtvig looked depressed.

"My daughter has cleaned it. I did not expect her tonight, you understand. I told her I was awaiting visitors, in the hope of getting rid . . . of reminding her she need not stay. Instead, she cleaned the house." He sighed.

Elizabeth was beginning to understand why Grundtvig had seemed envious of Margaret's free and giddy lifestyle. He was firmly under his daughter's efficient thumb, subject to her cleaning fits and her fussing over his health. No wonder he sympathized with Margaret's rebellion against her son.

But when they were seated, the capable police officer replaced the harassed father. "Tell me," he said simply.

Christian proceeded to do so. He omitted nothing, not even his ignominious encounters with the very large man in the knitted cap. Grundtvig listened with absorbed attention. The only time he betrayed emotion was when Christian mentioned the bullet that had so narrowly missed him.

"But that is—that is frightful!" he exclaimed, anger crimsoning his face. "When I get my hands on those rascals ... Go on, Christian, go on."

Elizabeth found this demonstration of paternal distress rather touching. Christian did not particularly care for it. There was a frosty tone in his voice when he resumed his narrative, which concluded on a high note, with the arrival of the severed finger. Dramatically he presented Grundtvig with the box.

"Good God," Grundtvig muttered, peering into the container. "Is it ...?"

"I don't think so." Christian summarized his reasoning on that subject. Grundtvig nodded respectfully.

"Very good, very good. I agree. It resembles an anatomical specimen. From a cadaver at a hospital, perhaps."

"Then one of the gang must be a medical student or a doctor," Elizabeth exclaimed.

"Quite possibly." Grundtvig smiled at her. "But it isn't much of a clue, is it? There are hundreds of doctors and medical students in Denmark, not to mention laboratory assistants and others who might have access to a dead body. However," he went on, forestalling Christian's attempt to speak, "that is not the immediate problem. We must persuade Margaret to return. She may be in serious trouble."

"May be?" Christian repeated. "I've been candid with you, Grundtvig; how about doing the same for me? You know something about this business or you wouldn't have reacted as you did when I called."

Grundtvig leaned forward till his face was only a few inches from Christian's. "My young friend, you must trust me. I know less than you think, and what little I know I cannot divulge. You understand; it is a question of . . . of . . ."

"National security," Elizabeth said breathlessly.

"Precisely." Grundtvig beamed at her.

"I don't give a damn about national security," Christian snapped. "I want to find Margaret."

"So do I. Believe me, nothing is more important to me at this moment than locating my old friend. You have not the faintest idea where she might be? She has not been in touch with you?"

"Not since Roskilde," Elizabeth said.

"And no way of reaching her? She would return if she thought you needed her." He continued to look at Christian.

"What do you suggest I do?" asked the latter bitingly. "Get myself shot or hit by a car so it makes the headlines? I don't know how to contact her."

"That seems a trifle extreme," Grundtvig said, his eyes twinkling. "You have no other ideas?"

"Only that I keep that appointment tonight."

"That would be absolutely insane," Elizabeth exclaimed. "You agree, don't you, Mr. Grundtvig?"

Grundtvig was silent for a moment; his eyes moved from one of them to the other. Then he said, "Not insane—no. Someone should keep that appointment. But Christian ought not risk himself. Perhaps—you, Miss Jones."

"What?" Christian jumped to his feet, his face crimson. "Why, you stupid old . . . Excuse me, but that is really the most idiotic idea I've ever heard. Absolutely out of the question. I won't permit it." And then, as Elizabeth's heart began to flutter with tender emotion, he turned a malignant scowl on her and added, "She'd screw it up somehow."

"Well, perhaps it was a stupid idea," Grundtvig said mildly. "While you are on your feet, my boy, could I trouble you to fetch some beer? It is in the refrigerator."

Christian looked as if he wanted to object, but good manners prevailed. He stamped out of the room, letting the kitchen door swing shut behind him.

Grundtvig turned to Elizabeth with a broad smile. "I was only joking, my dear. But you would have gone, wouldn't you?"

"I guess so. I'm stupid enough to do it."

"No, you are not stupid. You care about them. Not only Margaret, but Christian. You care very much."

"He's a rude, conceited, arrogant man," Elizabeth said.

"Ah, but love is not logical. I think you love him. I don't know why you do. I agree that he can be very exasperating. But you do. And," Grundtvig added, "he cares for you."

"No, he doesn't."

"Then why did he become so angry when I suggested you take the post of danger?" The door opened, admitting Christian with a fistful of beer bottles. Grundtvig went on, without a change of tone, "I think that neither of you should keep that appointment; for I can see that neither would allow the other to go alone. I will myself keep it."

"You?" Christian exclaimed.

"Or I will send someone younger, not so fat," Grundtvig amended, with a chuckle. "Leave it in my hands, young Christian. I will telephone you later to tell you what, if anything, transpires. May I offer you a beer?"

Elizabeth shook her head. Her dresses were getting tight around the waist in spite of all the running around she had been doing.

"No," Christian said. "Not unless you have something more to tell us."

"I thought we would talk pleasantly of life and love and art," Grundtvig murmured.

"That sounds charming. But perhaps we had better get back to the hotel."

"Very well." Grundtvig abandoned his casual air. "That might be best. And if you will take an old idiot's advice, you will stay in the hotel. Do not wander the dark streets, young Christian."

"I tell you, he does it on purpose, to annoy me," Christian muttered, as they walked toward the car.

Elizabeth turned to wave at the rotund figure silhouetted in the open doorway. Grundtvig was making sure they reached the car safely.

"I think he's sweet. You can't blame him, Christian. He is a policeman, after all. If this is a security matter—"

Christian slammed the car door with unnecessary force. "It's amazing how people crumple up and retreat when that magic word is mentioned. He was just trying to put us off."

He glanced out the side window, preparing to make a left turn. Suddenly he jerked the wheel around and brought the car screeching to a halt somewhere in the vicinity of the curb.

"There she is," he shouted, wrenching the door open. "Over there. Quick, don't let her get away!"

As Elizabeth stared, too surprised to move, he set off in hot pursuit of a bowed figure muffled in a dark cloak and hood. His quarry turned a startled face in his direction and then began to run with an agility and speed that contrasted impressively with its former hobbling progress. The features had been shadowed by the hood, but the person pursued was undoubtedly the proud possessor of a fine upstanding Roman nose.

Elizabeth got out and joined the chase. Christian's long legs enabled him to catch up with the cloaked figure before it reached the next intersection. He swept it into a close and not very affectionate embrace, despite its frantic efforts to resist. It began to yell.

The pitch was somewhere between bass and baritone. Christian promptly released his captive. The hood had fallen back in their struggle, and Elizabeth was horrified to behold the bald head and unfamiliar features of an infuriated old man. He began to beat Christian over the head with the cane he was carrying.

Christian retreated as Elizabeth advanced. They met ten feet away from the former captive, who was jumping up and down and making threatening gestures. Instinctively they clung to one another.

"How could you have made such a mistake?" Elizabeth gasped. She was torn between laughter and consternation.

"I'm starting to see her everywhere," Christian answered hysterically. "Hey, look out." The elderly gentleman had gained courage from Christian's retreat. He advanced on them, brandishing his cane.

"I'm sorry," Christian shouted. "Excuse me . . . uh . . . *undskyld* . . . Damn, I seem to have forgotten all my Danish. *Er der nogen her, der taler engelsk*—no, that's not what I meant to say. . . damn!" He threw up his arms to protect his head.

The old man paused. Studying Christian contemptuously, he hurled a single word at him—obviously an epithet—and then turned and walked away. There was a distinct swagger in his step.

"What did he call you?" Elizabeth asked.

"I think the word means 'pervert,' " Christian said. "Let's get out of here."

Christian carried a souvenir of the encounter in a red welt across his cheek. He did not find this as amusing as Elizabeth did.

"But it's your only visible scar," she pointed out. "People trying to kill you all over the place, and all you have to show for it is a bruise made by an old man who thought you were—"

"I suppose you'd be happier if I had bleeding wounds all over my body," snarled Christian.

He was still sulking when they reached the hotel, and his discovery that there had been no messages while they were gone did not improve his evil mood. Elizabeth anticipated another long, tedious evening.

There wasn't even a movie on television, only a documentary that seemed to have something to do with the breeding habits of a species of small crab. And with crabs, Elizabeth reflected, it was hard to tell what they were actually doing.

She watched it anyway. She was too restless to read, and Christian was not inclined toward conversation. I wonder why I love him, she thought, finally admitting the truth she had tried to suppress until Grundtvig's amiable tactlessness had forced her to face it. It can't be because I yearn to be Margaret's daughter-in-law. I'm beginning to think that might be a rather onerous position. He can be nice when he wants to. Under his stiff manner there is humor and kindness and a becoming humility. . . . Damn Margaret. She's responsible for those hidden insecurities. But I guess it's not her fault that she's a superior human being.

In such depressing speculation the evening passed with stupefying slowness. By midnight Elizabeth was exhausted by boredom and would have gone to bed; but she knew she would not be able to sleep until they heard from Grundtvig. The meeting had been set for midnight—Christian had grudgingly admitted that much—so they could not expect to hear anything before twelve thirty at the earliest, probably much later.

When the telephone rang, they both jumped for it. Christian got there first. His tense expression relaxed, and he handed the phone to Elizabeth.

"It's for you. Sounds like that dizzy-looking receptionist."

The nasal tones were indeed unmistakable. The girl apologized for calling so late. "But I'm going home now, miss, and I just noticed there was a letter come for you. It must of got in the wrong box. It's from New York, so maybe it's important."

"Does the envelope say 'Frenchton and Monk'?" Elizabeth asked. The deduction was not difficult; her employers were the only persons in New York who knew her present address.

"Yes, that's the name."

"I'll come down and get it." Elizabeth explained the situation to Christian, adding wryly, "I suppose it's a series of admonitions to be kind to Margaret. If they only knew!"

"Why not leave it till morning?"

"It's something to do." Elizabeth added, "I have not found the evening's entertainment all that exciting."

Christian refused to be provoked. "Don't go out of the hotel."

"Why would I do that? Anyhow, Grundtvig meant that warning for you. Nobody wants me."

She hadn't intended to express it quite that way. She left the room before Christian could reply.

The residents of the hotel were not given to late hours or raucous parties. The lobby was dim and quiet when she emerged from the lift. She went to the office and opened the door.

And that was all she knew, until she woke up to find herself lying on a hard mattress in a strange room with a headache that seemed about to split her skull.

🥀 9 🥀

DAZEDLY Elizabeth contemplated the ceiling. It was the only thing she dared contemplate; her first attempt to move had brought on a wave on intense dizziness and nausea. The ceiling had very little of interest. It was plain white plaster, neatly patched and repaired in several places. From it dangled a brass chain supporting a bare light bulb.

When the dizziness had subsided, Elizabeth cautiously tried to move her arms. They responded, but not well; they kept flopping back onto the bed, or onto her chest, every time she lifted them. At any rate, they were there. That was something.

Next she tried her feet. One worked all right. When she shifted the other, a jangling sound and a feeling of constriction followed. Unwarily she raised her head to look. There was an iron band around one ankle, and a chain attached to the band. Where the other end of the chain went she did not know. Nausea swept over her again and she let her head fall back. There seemed to be no point in staying awake, so she lost consciousness.

The second time she awoke matters had improved somewhat. She was still lying on the hard mattress, but the sick feeling was gone. Slowly she raised herself to a sitting position and subjected her surroundings to a careful scrutiny.

The room was small, painfully clean and painfully bare. The only object in it was the bed. No rugs, no ornaments, no pictures on the wall. There had been pictures; squares of slightly lighter paint showed where they had hung.

The ceiling sloped steeply down on one side of the room. There was a single window in that sloping wall. It was covered by heavy planks. The only light came from the bulb, which glared in her eyes.

Elizabeth turned her attention to the chain. Its far end, the one that was not attached to her ankle, disappeared over the foot of the bed, which was constructed, apparently for eternity, of heavy dark wood. Slowly Elizabeth got to her feet. She felt better. Lightheaded and dizzy and very empty, but better.

She expected that the chain would be secured to the bedpost, and that she might eventually hope to free herself by lifting or breaking the post. This expedient, she soon learned, was ruled out by the fact that the chain had been wound in and around the posts and footboard and secured by a heavy padlock.

Hearing a sound at the door, Elizabeth hopped back onto the bed and huddled against the headboard. When the door opened she was neither surprised nor pleased to see the familiar visage of Mr. Schmidt.

He gave her a casual uninterested glance and then spoke to someone behind him. "She's awake."

He stepped back—the door was too narrow to admit more than a single person—and another man appeared. Elizabeth had never seen him before. On the whole she preferred his face to Schmidt's. It was a flat, rather bovine countenance, with heavy lines dragging the mouth into a reverse curve; but the resulting expression was sad rather than vicious. If she had seen him in other surroundings she would have taken him for a carpenter or bricklayer, worried about his finances and his children's escapades, but essentially harmless. He wore working clothes—a heavy cotton shirt and khaki pants—hence her instinctive identification with manual labor rather than office work. His hands bore out the idea, being large and calloused. He had to stoop to enter the room.

While Schmidt leaned against the door, watching, the other man plodded toward the bed. He avoided Elizabeth's eyes. One hand reached for her ankle.

She pulled it away. His roughened skin and torn nails, the sheer size of his fingers, filled her with terror. As he leaned toward her she became aware of a strange sour smell, faint but repugnant.

Instead of making a grab for her, as Schmidt probably would have done, he stepped back and held up a key.

"You come," he said. "Wash, eat. Not—not . . . "

His English gave out at that intriguing point, but the mildness of his voice and the inducements he had offered relieved Elizabeth's fear. Schmidt let out a nasty laugh. "If you prefer my company to Eric's, just say so, honey."

"I don't," Elizabeth said. It was the first time she had tried to speak. Her voice was rusty and weak, but she was pleased to note that it showed no trace of fear. She offered her ankle to Eric, who was holding the key high, like a talisman. His big chapped hands were surprisingly gentle. He unlocked the iron band and made an awkward gesture toward the door. "Come. Wash. Eat."

Elizabeth followed him. Schmidt stood aside just enough to let her pass. The door was narrow, but she thought he purposely placed himself so she had to brush by him. However, he made no attempt to touch her.

Outside was a small landing, with another door opposite the one through which she had come. A steep staircase led down. Eric preceded her, indicating with a gesture that she should hold the handrail. The steps were narrow and the slope was extreme, more like a ladder than a staircase.

The primitiveness and poverty of the room she had seen thus far had led her to expect little in the way of sanitary conveniences. She was pleased to find that the bathroom had modern plumbing. It did not have a lock on the door. Elizabeth turned her attention to her immediate necessities.

Cool water splashed on her face and arms restored her to near normalcy. Leaving the water running in the basin, she turned to the window, which was covered by a cheap plastic curtain. She had no intention of trying to escape; Schmidt would be in the room instantly if there was a sound of glass breaking or the window being raised, but it would be advantageous to learn as much as she could about the place where she was imprisoned.

When she raised a corner of the curtain her hopes plummeted. The window was thick, opaque glass and the frame had been screwed shut. The screws shone brightly, obviously new.

"Come out or I'll come in," Schmidt called.

Elizabeth obeyed at once. There was no sense in being belligerent or defiant; in fact, she regretted her first sharp reply to Schmidt. If they thought she was terrified, they would be more inclined to relax their guard. It wasn't much of a plan, but it was the best she could do at the moment.

She had hoped to see more of the lower floor of the house, but the other doors leading from the hall were closed, and instead of taking her to the kitchen Eric indicated that she should go back upstairs. He followed her with a tray, which he had procured while she was in the bathroom. After glancing around the room as if in search of a piece of furniture that was no longer there, he shrugged and put the tray on the bed.

Schmidt made a sweeping gesture, in mocking imitation of a headwaiter. "Enjoy your lunch, lady."

"I . . . I'd rather wait till I'm alone," Elizabeth murmured.

"No dice, sweetheart. Eat, or Papa will take it away. Makes no difference to me."

The tray had been covered with a white cloth, an incongruously housewifely touch. Elizabeth removed it. Underneath was a thick white china bowl filled with a soupy concoction that was probably meant to be stew; she could see chunks of meat and some scorched potatoes. There was also a bottle of beer and a few ragged slices of heavy dark bread.

The beer struck a questionable note, but Elizabeth was still extremely thirsty. There had been no glass or cup in the bathroom, and the amount of water that can be carried to the lips in cupped hands is limited. She drank some of the beer and then turned her attention to the stew, using the only implement on the tray, a large spoon. She had not expected gourmet food, but the first mouthful made her grimace. Not only was the seasoning vile—too little salt, too much of another spice she could not identify—but the potatoes had definitely been burned.

"Lousy, isn't it?" Schmidt said, genuine emotion coloring his voice. "As a cook Eric stinks."

Eric shot a mildly resentful glance at his cohort, and Elizabeth wondered how much English he understood. More than he spoke, perhaps. Not that it made any difference to her; Eric was obviously part of the gang, and perhaps his disposition was fully as unpleasant as Schmidt's. A mild face and quiet manner do not guarantee virtue.

She ate the bread and forced down a few more bites of stew, thinking she might need her strength—though at the moment she could not imagine what for. Then she smiled apologetically at Eric.

"It's very good, but I'm not hungry. Thank you."

Eric made no response whatever to this ingratiating remark. He stood like a statue, staring at the floor, until Schmidt said impatiently, "Lock her up again and take the tray, you moron."

Eric obeyed. He understood English; he simply chose not to understand Elizabeth. She did not regret her attempt to be conciliatory. A prisoner is bound to test all possible weaknesses in the opposition. The chance of persuading him to help her seemed exceedingly remote—for one thing, Schmidt had been careful never to leave them alone—but it couldn't do any harm to try.

"See you later, sweetheart," Schmidt said.

"Wait—please." Elizabeth's resolution failed at the idea of being locked in for an indeterminate period, alone and ignorant of what was happening. "What are you going to do with me?"

"Nothing at all, sweetheart. Not that I wouldn't like to do something with you."

His expression reminded her of the Nazi officer's leer. She thought of encouraging that interest, but the idea was too repellent. Not even to escape would she submit to Schmidt's touch. And it probably wouldn't do any good. Schmidt was not the type to wax sentimental over any woman.

He was watching her expectantly, so she gave him what she assumed he wanted—a whimpering voice and quivering lower lip.

"Where am I? What do you want? How long do I have to stay here?"

"Until we get what we want. If you don't know what that is, there's no point in telling you."

He started to close the door.

"Can't I at least have something to read?" Elizabeth moaned. "I'll go crazy if I have to sit here hour after hour with nothing to do."

"Well, I'll see what I can find. Better take a nap. It helps pass the time."

He grinned unpleasantly and shut the door. She heard the rattle of the key in the lock.

It was such a relief to be rid of his jeering presence that the room seemed almost friendly. Elizabeth made herself as comfortable as she could, but she did not lie down. She didn't want to go to sleep. She had to think.

Go back to the beginning—to the previous night. Had it been the previous night, or longer? She had no way of knowing. She was not wearing a wristwatch. But Schmidt had said something about lunch. That might have been deliberate misdirection, but there was no reason for him to care whether she knew what day it was.

Assume, then, that something over twelve hours had passed since she had fallen into the simple-minded but highly successful trap. It could hardly fail; not only was she unprepared for trouble within the hotel, but neither she nor Christian had believed there was any threat to her. She had always been the innocent bystander.

I might have known, she thought ruefully. It's usually the innocent bystander who gets axed.

No question but that the trap had been set for her; the receptionist had asked for her specifically. Was the girl a member of the gang, or had she been held at gunpoint and forced to make the call by the kidnapper? He must have been behind the door when I walked into the office, Elizabeth thought. She explored her head. Yes, she had a bump; not a very big one; it was about the same size and shape as the one Christian had acquired in the museum. The meager little man was indeed an expert at his trade. Only long practice could enable him to produce bumps of the same size and shape on several different heads.

Then a drug of some kind? Most probably. A blow that light would not have kept her unconscious for long, or made her feel so sick and dizzy.

It all made sense, thus far, but it didn't contribute much. She had no idea where she was—or why.

A wave of despondency washed over her. Resolutely she fought it off. Speculation about motives and meanings was a waste of time. She and Christian had done too much of that already, and this latest development only added confusion to chaos. She must concentrate on a means of escape.

Her reading, and her exposure to the visual media, had been more varied than she cared to admit. Intellectuals were not supposed to revel in *The Count of Monte Cristo* and *The Scarlet Pimpernel*, or watch thrillers on television. During her college days Elizabeth had been enough of a snob to conceal her interest in lowbrow entertainment; many a lurid paperback had been thrust under a chair or sat upon when a friend dropped in unexpectedly. Now she was glad she had never abandoned her fictional heroes. It would be funny if the despised thrillers proved more useful than the literary classics. She leaned against the headboard and tried to remember the stories she had read about prisons and escapes therefrom.

Basically, escape methods fell into two categories. The first was physical and direct—cutting one's way through the stone walls and iron bars that, despite the poet, do indeed a prison make. The second method was to overcome the jailer—by persuasion, bribery and corruption, seduction, or force.

She got off the bed and unreeled the chain to its full length. The slack was a good ten feet. Apparently they didn't mind if she walked around the room. Brisk exercise would not be feasible, however; the chain was quite heavy. Dragging it behind her, she went to the door.

It was the most obvious exit, but it was not the most practical; even if she could open it, she would have to get out of a house whose floor plan was unknown to her—without being caught by Schmidt and/or his ally. The idea of suddenly coming upon Schmidt as she crept down the stairs made her cringe. She was, therefore, not too distressed to find that the door appeared to be impregnable. The lock was a massive old-fashioned mechanism of cast iron. The door itself was solid wood, not a flimsy modern construction of hollow panels.

Draping the chain artistically over one arm, she made a circuit of the room. It didn't take long. The door was in the center of one of the short sides, the bed in the center of the other. One of the long walls was a solid blank. When she thumped on the plastered surface, she heard only a dull thud.

The other wall sloped down almost to the floor. The single window was in this wall. Obviously her prison was in the attic or top floor of the house. That meant that even if she could open the window she would be high above the ground—two, possibly three stories up.

All the same, the window was better than the door. Elizabeth examined the boards that covered it.

There were three of them, each three-quarters of an inch thick. Heavy screws held them fixed to the window frame.

If only she had a piece of metal—a nail file, a knife, even the spoon that had been served with the terrible stew. Schmidt wasn't taking any chances. He had watched her every move. He had not even let her keep the beer bottle. Elizabeth admitted to herself that he need not have worried. A beer bottle could make a nasty weapon, but she wasn't the girl to use it—not even on Schmidt.

One glance at the floor eliminated that as a means of exit. The bare boards were old and warped, but the cracks had been neatly filled. If only the Danes weren't such neat people! If only they didn't build their houses so solidly! She felt sure she could have clawed her way out of any modern American domicile with her bare hands.

Elizabeth went back to the bed and lay down. The chain was more of an encumbrance than she had anticipated. It had left red imprints on her arm.

She ran down her list of great escape stories. The Thinking Machine, in the classic tale, had managed to reach a confederate on the outside of the prison via an old disused sewer and an accommodating rat, which he had caught and trained to run down the sewer carrying a message. Elizabeth snorted. To think that once she had admired that author's ingenuity! He had invented the sewer and put it right where it was needed. She had no such convenience, and if she encountered a rat, nothing on earth could force her to touch it.

The Count of Monte Cristo was of no help whatsoever. Monte Cristo's fellow prisoner, the old Abbé, had spent twenty years—or some such depressing figure—chiseling through the stone wall, and then had ended up in the wrong place. She didn't have twenty years—or a spoon that could be sharpened into a chisel—or a stone to sharpen it on.

The Scarlet Pimpernel, imprisoned by his deadly enemy Chauvelin, had been in a situation more analogous to hers. Chauvelin, cruel agent of the French Revolution, wanted to recapture the little Dauphin, whom the gallant Pimpernel had freed some weeks earlier. Feigning surrender, the Pimpernel had persuaded Chauvelin that he alone could lead the pursuers to the Dauphin's hiding place. Once outside the prison, he had made good his escape, though guarded by an entire troop of soldiers.

Elizabeth sighed. It was an ingenious idea, and she might have tried it if she had had the faintest notion what Schmidt wanted. She could hardly offer to lead him to . . . whatever it was . . . unless she knew *what* it was. (Margaret's bathrobe? Nonsense.) Besides, if Schmidt believed her claim, he might decide to force the information from her. The Scarlet Pimpernel had heroically resisted Chauvelin's torture for weeks before pretending to succumb. Not me, Elizabeth thought. One touch of the thumbscrew or the whip, and I'd tell him everything I knew—which is nothing—which could lead to extremely unpleasant consequences if he didn't believe I knew nothing.

She was glad she had thought about it before she tried it.

In one movie she had seen the hero pretended illness. When his jailer rushed in, in response to his howls of agony, the hero had hit him on the head . . . That wouldn't work either. She didn't even have a beer bottle.

How about bribery? She had no money and no jewelry, but perhaps she could tell Schmidt she would wire for funds. After all, her father was a millionaire—chairman of General Motors . . . and she was a world-famous poet. Schmidt wouldn't dare keep her prisoner. The whole Danish police department, and Interpol, and the French Foreign Legion were looking for her. A good thing she had studied karate. When he advanced on her, leering from ear to ear, she shouted, "*Hiya!*" and kicked him in the groin. He fell writhing to the floor. The cavalry was coming. She could hear the bugles . . .

She awoke with a start and a gasp when the key rattled in the lock. The shattering of her dream was so painful that tears welled up in her eyes. She brushed them away with the back of her hand, forgetting that she had meant to play the sniveling female.

Schmidt and Eric appeared, and the original performance of bathroom and tray was repeated. But there was one difference. The opaque window in the bathroom was darker than it had been the first time.

The stew was even worse warmed over. Elizabeth put her spoon down after the first bite. "I can't live on bread and beer," she protested.

"It won't be for long," Schmidt said.

This could be an encouraging comment or the exact opposite. Elizabeth decided not to ask what Schmidt meant. In this case ignorance could be bliss.

She ate every crumb of the bread and finished the beer. Beer was very nourishing. Then she smiled at Eric.

"I can't eat any more. I'm sorry."

For the first time he looked directly at her. His eyes were a soft faded blue and as expressionless as glass marbles.

"She says she can't eat that swill," Schmidt shouted. "I don't blame her. It stinks. Take it away. No more. You hear me? Take it away."

"You've hurt his feelings," Elizabeth said. She continued to beam determinedly at Eric, who paid no attention to her, but moved to carry out Schmidt's orders. When he bent to relock the iron band she got another whiff of the strange pungent odor and wondered what it could be. Neither Eric's clothes nor his person looked dirty; though his hands bore stains of oil or paint, or some other substance impervious to soap and water, they had obviously been washed quite recently. His fingertips were pink and wrinkled.

"Don't bother trying to charm him," Schmidt said, as Eric walked out carrying the tray. "He's slow. If you're thinking of seducing a jailer, how about me?"

"I'd rather have something to read," Elizabeth said. "You promised you'd look."

It was much easier to sound plaintive and frightened than she had expected—and this frightened her even more. She had read of prisoners who came to identify with and depend on their captors, to such an extent that they sometimes begged to be permitted to join the gang. She had never been able to understand how that could happen. Hate and fear and resentment surely could not metamorphose into affection. Now she wondered. Would long days or weeks of imprisonment have that effect on her?

Her pleading voice pleased Schmidt. "Okay," he said tolerantly. "I'll have a look."

When he came back he had a handful of magazines and a paperback book. He tossed these at the bed. Several of the magazines fell on the floor, and Schmidt stood waiting until Elizabeth, divining what he wanted, climbed off the bed and knelt to retrieve them. Schmidt did not comment. After watching her with a faint smile he went out and locked the door.

Still kneeling, Elizabeth turned her face to the door and addressed it in a stream of profanity whose richness and inventiveness surprised her. She felt a little foolish swearing at a door, but there was no doubt she felt much better when she was finished. Then she climbed onto the bed and examined her reading material.

It consisted of several magazines, all in Danish. One appeared to be a news magazine. The subject matter of the others eluded her until she came upon a photograph of a big, snobbish-looking bull. Danish farm journals—that's what tney were. Fascinating reading, even if they had been in English.

Disgustedly she tossed them aside and picked up the paperback book. At least it was in English. The cover depicted a half-naked female cowering before a man standing over her with a whip. The title was *Dead Drab in a Ditch*.

Just the sort of literature she would have expected Schmidt to read. She was tempted to heave it across the room. But, having slept half the day, she was now wide awake. It was Danish cows or American drabs or nothing.

In desperation she returned to the news magazine, hoping it might have pictures. It did; and she amused herself—to use the term loosely—trying to deduce the subject matter of the articles from the illustrations. She concluded that the periodical was at least two weeks old. The major news stories concerned matters she had read about before she left the States.

The magazines were additional proof of a fact she had already suspected from the vile food. There was no woman in the house. Schmidt's sense of humor was direct and unsubtle; he would not deliberately select from journals and avoid women's magazines if any of the latter had been available.

The confirmation of what had been only a half-realized premise made her feel very lonely. The female of the species can be as vicious as the male; but if Elizabeth fell ill, or injured herself, she would be dependent on the men for care. It was not a pleasant thought.

She forced herself to think of something else. The magazines suggested another idea. Surely only a farmer would subscribe to journals about cows. Had she been taken clear out of Copenhagen, into the country?

Trailing her chain, she went to the window and pressed her ear against the boards. They were certainly thick, but were they heavy enough to keep out all sound? She heard nothing. Surely the roar of traffic or the sound of a siren or horn would come through.

The exercise reminded her of one sense she had not yet fully employed—her hearing. She tried the door first and was rewarded by a remote ringing sound that she finally identified as the pulsation of her own heartbeat. Then she lay down on the floor and put her ear against the boards.

At first she heard nothing. She was about to get up when she caught a thudding noise, possibly caused by a closing door. The faintest, most distant murmur of voices followed. Elizabeth pressed her head against the wood till her ear ached, but she was unable to make out distinct words.

"Damn," she said. Trudging back to the bed, clanking like Marley's ghost, she reached for *Dead Drab in a Ditch*.

It wasn't quite as awful as she had expected. But it was pretty bad.

"Mitch Gruber shoved his creaking swivel chair away from his beat-up desk and got the bottle of absinthe out of the bottom drawer. He raised it to his lips. The fiery liquid burned a path clear down to . . . "

"I don't think that's possible," Elizabeth muttered. She went on reading.

Mitch was a private eye. She had deduced that right away, because of the bottle of booze in the desk drawer. The inevitable sultry blonde entered on page two. Mitch kissed her passionately on page four. On page six somebody shot her through the window—and the guts—and she collapsed in a pool of gore.

Even sex and violence can be boring when carried to excess—as they usually are. By page seventy-six, Elizabeth's eyelids began to droop. The fourth murder (decapitation) made her yawn. Four pages later she was sound asleep.

For the second time that day the sound of the key in the lock brought her awake. She sat up, rubbing her eyes. Had she been asleep that long? If her theories about time were accurate, the next meal ought to be breakfast. Hopefully it would not consist of another batch of burned stew.

The door opened and Elizabeth saw not Schmidt's familiar face, but Eric's not so familiar back. This was enough of a change in routine to awaken her completely and inspire a thrill of alarm, which intensified as Eric backed slowly into the room. He was a large man and the doorway was narrow; he was all the way in the room before Elizabeth understood the reason for his unconventional method of locomotion. He was carrying something—or rather, one end of it. Schmidt followed, carrying the other end. This consisted of a pair of rather large feet and two legs clad in trousers that had once been light brown; they were now thickly coated with mud, dust, and berry stains. Eric's body concealed the upper portion of this apparition, but Elizabeth would have known the feet anywhere. With a shriek of horror she rolled off the bed, and the chain jangled an atmospherically gothic accompaniment.

✢ 10 ✢

As soon as he was in the room, Schmidt let go of Christian's feet, which hit the floor with a crash. Eric lowered his portion of the load less precipitately and stepped out of the way as Elizabeth flung herself upon her fallen rescuer.

He now had two bumps on his head—neat, symmetrical bumps whose contours proclaimed their creator as a fat pink nude goddess announces, "Rubens!" There did not appear to be anything else wrong with him. He was breathing heavily through his nose, and the frantic hands she ran over his face and body found nothing that should not have been there.

"You rotten bastard," she said.

"That's not a nice thing to say," Schmidt remarked. "He went to a lot to trouble to find you."

"I was talking to you."

"I figured you were. Well, sweetheart, so long for now. At least you'll have somebody to entertain you—if you can wake him up."

"I need water, bandages—"

"Too bad."

A rumble of unintelligible comment from Eric stopped Schmidt on his way to the door. Apparently it was an appeal, for Schmidt said grudgingly, "Oh, all right, get her some water. Hurry up. This is one hell of a complication, and I've got things to do."

Eric was soon back with a plastic container of water. He and Schmidt departed, leaving Elizabeth free to express her feelings.

She did so with abandon, forgetting her plans for first aid. When Christian opened his eyes she didn't notice, she was crying so hard. A tear fell straight down onto one of his eyeballs, and he protested feebly.

"Ouch. That stings."

"I'm sorry."

"Crying isn't going to help, you know."

He sounded normal—irritated, querulous, critical. Elizabeth sat back on her heels and beamed at him, wiping her eyes with her fingers. Christian sat up. He reached into his pocket and presented her with a large clean white handkerchief.

"Are you all right?" he inquired.

Elizabeth peered at him over the handkerchief. "No, I'm not all right. I'm frightened and confused and mad and—"

"Did they hurt you?"

His tone was more urgent. Mollified, Elizabeth admitted, "No. I'm all right. Christian, how did they catch you?"

"I let them catch me. I practically forced them to. Kidnapping me was not part of their plan."

"You're talking nonsense."

"Let's get up off this hard floor." He rose and offered a hand to Elizabeth. She stood up, jangling, and then Christian saw the chain. A wave of angry red darkened his face.

"That filthy bastard Schmidt—"

"Now, now. Swearing won't help." Elizabeth looped the chain over her arm. His anger had pleased her enormously. "Come over to the bed. It's the only place to sit," she added hastily. "Except the floor."

"So I see." Christian's voice still shook with fury. "And you've been in this filthy hole since last night?"

"I don't even know what time it is." They sat down on the bed side by side, their shoulders touching.

Christian consulted his watch. "Five to one. A little over twenty-four hours. Elizabeth . . . Has it been very bad?"

The moment was fraught with emotion. Elizabeth was tempted to take advantage of the concern in his voice, to cast herself on his manly chest and whimper. She restrained herself. He would have expressed as much outrage if he had found a dog chained in a filthy kennel; and she had already made a sufficient fool of herself, dripping tears all over him.

"Mostly it's been boring," she said. "For heaven's sake tell me what has happened."

Christian lay back, his hands under his head. "Excuse me if I recline. I'm pooped. Didn't get any sleep last night."

"Oh, really. What were you doing?"

"Looking for you, of course. I waited five minutes; when you didn't come back, I went after you. Found the office closed and locked, and not a trace of you. I got Roger and Marie out of bed and we turned the place upside down. How did they get you away so fast?"

"Damned if I know. I walked into the office, and *bam!* that was it." She added, "My bump matches yours."

"Uh-huh. The little owner of the big trunk. He must be their hit man, or whatever it's called. The one that does the dirty work."

"He got you too?"

"All in good time," Christian said, still lying down. "I figured out, of course, that the receptionist was one of the gang—"

"Are you sure? She may have been forced to call me."

"If you'll stop interrupting, I'll tell you how I know. I started with the assumption that she was one of the bad guys. There were several substantiating facts, such as the peculiar illness that struck the staff of the hotel, and the fact that the former receptionist was the only one who didn't recover immediately. Besides, Roger swore the place was locked tight. It always is, at ten o'clock, and nobody could have broken in without setting off the alarms. So the kidnapper had to be admitted by someone on the inside."

"Not bad," Elizabeth said. She lay down beside Christian. "But there's one big fallacy in your train of—"

Christian raised his voice and continued, ignoring the objection. "The hardest part was waiting to see whether the wench would come to work the next afternoon—today, that is. I thought she might, even if she was guilty; so I beguiled the intervening hours with a few errands, including the one I thought they wanted me to do."

He rolled an encouraging eye in her direction, and she said obediently, "And what was that, master detective?"

"Publicizing your disappearance. What other reason would they have to snatch you except to put pressure on Margaret?"

"Now wait a minute. If they wanted Margaret to surrender herself—or whatever she has that they want—they would have kidnapped *you*. I'm sure she has only the most amiable feelings toward me, but she'd give in a lot faster if you were the one in danger."

"I think I've figured that out," Christian said complacently. "Kidnapping me wasn't all that easy. Besides being a fairly husky specimen, capable of defending myself against . . . Did you say something?"

"Who, me?"

"Oh. I thought you said . . . Well, aside from that, you stuck to me like a burr, and that presented something of a logistical problem. I don't know how much manpower they have, but I get the impression that this is a fairly small-scale operation—three or four people, maybe. Why should they risk the complications of trying to nab both of us when they could accomplish the same thing by snatching you? You were much more vulnerable because we didn't think you were in danger." He stopped suddenly, as if he had been about to say more but had decided not to. Then he resumed, "So I called Grundtvig and persuaded him to do the whole missing-persons bit—announcements, posters, rewards. By this time the word has gone out, and Margaret is bound to hear it. Incidentally, nobody turned up at the rendezvous last night. Grundtvig's man waited till one A.M."

"They were too busy with me," Elizabeth said. "That appointment was a fake."

"Possibly." Christian's voice lost some of its assurance. "Or maybe something happened to make them change their minds. Will you let me get on with the main theme? I had it neatly organized before you distracted me."

"Sorry."

"Anyway. Blondie was supposed to come on duty at four o'clock. Sure enough, at five minutes to the hour there she was, bright as a button and innocent as a lamb. She was shocked to hear that you were missing. She said she gave you your letter and you left, with a cheery good-night. She couldn't imagine what had happened to you. Maybe you had a late date or something?"

"That's exactly what she would say if she was innocent."

"Oh, it was a reasonable story," Christian conceded. "I might have believed it, if I had not known you would never have been stupid enough to stick your nose outside the door of the hotel.

"I did not follow my natural inclination, which was to slap the little liar silly. I pretended to believe her. When she took her dinner break I just happened to be getting in the car, and I offered her a lift. I headed straight for the outskirts of town. The tricky part was keeping her from jumping out when I had to stop for traffic lights and signals, but she was no more anxious for publicity than I was, and she is not a quick thinker; I made sure she stayed rattled until I was ready to stop. When I finally did, I let her have it. No," he added, with a sidelong glance at Elizabeth, "I didn't lay a hand on her. I just told her I was going to beat her brains out if she didn't tell me where you were."

"And she did?"

"Of course not. She's no novice. She knew I wasn't going to hurt her. No, my scheme was much more effective. I let her pull a gun on me and steal the car."

"Well, aren't you brilliant! Why didn't you just persuade her to shoot you?"

"She didn't want to shoot me, stupid. Nobody wants to shoot me. At least," Christian added, less confidently, "up till now nobody has wanted to shoot me. They want Margaret. I figured the worst Blondie could do was hit me on the head; and I'm getting sort of used to that. She didn't even go that far. I had picked a deserted street with no houses around, only factories and shops that were closed for the night. She made me get out of the car, and took off. I knew she wouldn't go back to the hotel, not with me on the loose, and I hoped she would head for the place where her confederates were holed up. If you weren't there, one of them would know where you were."

"But if she took the car, how did you—"

"Ah. That is where the real brilliance of the plan comes in. Earlier in the day I had rented a second car and had driven it to the spot I had selected. I waited till she turned the corner, hopped into my trusty rented Fiat, and roared off in pursuit."

He cocked an eye at her, expecting praise. Elizabeth didn't trust herself to speak for a while. Finally she said in a voice choked with emotion,"You deliberately followed her to the gang's hideout, knowing you would be caught, just to find me?"

"Well," Christian said reluctantly, "getting caught wasn't exactly . . . It was a last resort, you might say."

"That is the most idiotic plan I ever heard of! I don't suppose you had the sense to tell Grundtvig what you were up to?"

Christian sat up, glaring. "If that's the thanks I get—"

"Thanks for what? Now they've got both of us."

A gloomy silence descended. Elizabeth was regretting her harsh words but didn't know how to apologize. Christian was unable to counter the logic of her complaint.

"Do you have any idea where we are?" Elizabeth asked finally.

"Of course I know. I drove here, didn't I?"

"Oh, you mean you got all the way to your destination before they grabbed you?"

"I don't know why I should tell you anything. All you do is bitch and make sarcastic remarks."

"I'm sorry. Really. I guess I'm not in a very good mood right now."

Christian's face relaxed into the smile that was his most engaging feature—rueful, youthful, apologetic. "You have reason to be depressed. I'm the one who should apologize. I goofed. But all is not lost. I even anticipated this."

"Tell me all about it, you wonderful person."

"If you insist." Christian stretched out again. "Well, I followed the wench and my car onto the highway going west— the same one we took to Roskilde. The first part was a piece of cake; there was enough traffic to make me unobtrusive. The trouble began when we passed Roskilde and turned off onto a side road. After a while her car and mine were the only ones in sight. I didn't dare get too far back for fear of losing her. Finally she turned off onto a private road, hardly more than a lane, and I went roaring past with what I hoped was a convincing imitation of a homeward-bound farmer. It was still daylight. This damned late twilight makes criminal activities difficult."

"I went on for about a mile, just to play safe, left the car by the road, and came back. It was a superb performance, if I do say so. I used every trick I could remember out of Fenimore Cooper and the Hardy Boys. I got scratched crawling under brambles and soaked my feet crossing a stream or two. It was beginning to get dark when I sneaked up the lane and found myself in a farmyard."

"So it is a farm. I deduced that."

"I won't ask how, because this is my turn to show off," Christian said firmly. "I hid in a shed until it was fully dark. Then I investigated the house. It's a small place, only four rooms downstairs and an attic above. I suppose that's where we are now, in the attic.

"There was a light in one room, which proved to be the kitchen. The curtains were drawn and I could only see a small part of the room—a sink and one corner of a table. But the window was open. I heard everything."

"I recognized Schmidt's voice and knew I had hit pay dirt. He was yelling at the blonde. Somewhat to my surprise the basis of his complaint seemed to be her refusal to cook."

Elizabeth laughed. "If you knew what the food has been like, you'd understand. Go on."

"She said she hadn't hired out as a domestic. Every now and then I'd hear a kind of rumbling noise—a third person talking in Danish, expostulating with both of them and trying to calm them down. When he said something, the other two both yelled at him to shut up."

"The role of the peacemaker," Elizabeth murmured.

"It was the damnedest conversation for a pack of crooks," Christian said. "And the most frustrating. I didn't want to hear about their domestic problems. I wanted to find out whether you were in the house. Finally Schmidt got down to cases. 'Now I've got to telephone,' he said. 'He isn't going to like this, Cheryl.' She said tough, or words to that effect, and added that she was no longer needed at the hotel anyway."

"I was getting very interested in the conversation. That was one of my mistakes. Also, I was squatting; the window is low to the ground, and I didn't want to take a chance on being seen. My legs got cramped. When the light caught me I didn't move fast enough."

"Car lights?"

"It was a bicycle, actually. That's why I didn't hear it coming. But it had a very powerful headlight. When the rider saw me, he let out a yell. Everybody came boiling out of the house and away we went, me staggering with cramps and the rest of them spry as distance runners. I'd have gotten away, though, if the damned dog hadn't started to bark. I had concluded there was no dog. It was one of the first things I looked for when I made my preliminary reconnaissance, and I was a little surprised not to see one. They had it shut up in a shed on the other side of the house. They had lost sight of me in the darkness by the time I got to the shed; but the dog heard me and cut loose. They grabbed me when I tried to climb the fence. The little guy hit me; and that was it."

"So," Elizabeth said. "Here we are."

"Schmidt seemed annoyed at your turning up."

"It does complicate matters for them. They've no way of letting Margaret know I've been caught, and no way of receiving communications from her."

"They could leave a message for her at the hotel. She may come back when she learns I've been kidnapped."

"I refuse to solve their problems for them," Christian said drowsily. "Let them worry about it."

"Are you going to sleep?" Elizabeth rose on one elbow and peered into his face. He blinked and swallowed a yawn.

"I had better not. We have work to do."

"There's no way out of here," Elizabeth said despondently. "Unless you happened to bring a gun and a screwdriver and an ax."

"It just so happens . . . " He sat up and searched his pockets. "No, the gun is gone. I figured they would find that."

"You had a gun?" Elizabeth exclaimed. "How did you—"

"With great difficulty. This is a law-abiding country. I meant it as a decoy, actually. Thought it might distract them from a thorough search. *Voilà . . . !*" He pulled up his pants leg. Strapped to his calf was an empty scabbard.

Christian's face fell. "Damn. I hoped they would miss the knife."

"Not with Schmidt holding you by the feet."

"Oh, well." Christian took off his jacket and unbuttoned his shirt. Rows of adhesive tape had been lavishly applied to his chest and stomach, which bulged with oddly shaped lumps. Christian began removing the tape, wincing with each tug. "Next time I'll use more gauze and less tape," he muttered.

From under the tape came a pocket knife, a strange-looking instrument with a hook on one end and a point on the other, a tiny flashlight, and a ball-point pen. Christian stared blankly at the last. "I wonder how that got in there."

"Maybe you were a little upset," Elizabeth suggested gently.

"Maybe."

"What's that?" She indicated the hooked instrument.

"A picklock."

"Do you know how to use it?"

"I understand the general principle. But we'll try the screwdriver first. The window is our best bet. I know what's out there, and I have no idea what we can expect to encounter beyond the door."

"Schmidt, Eric, the blonde, the hit man—"

"As I said, the window is our best bet."

The pocket knife was one of the elaborate Swiss types with every possible amenity, including a corkscrew and an ivory toothpick.

"You never know when you'll need one of those," Elizabeth remarked.

Christian tossed the toothpick aside. "The screwdriver might be more useful in this case."

It was, of course, totally inadequate for the job at hand, but he managed to loosen two of the screws before it broke.

"Why didn't I bring a regulation size?" Christian muttered.

"You didn't know you would need one. You selected an all-purpose tool; I think that was very clever."

Christian grunted. He pulled out the shortest and stoutest of the knife blades and went on with his work. It was not the most convenient of tools for the purpose. His hands were bleeding from a dozen small cuts before he loosened the third screw. At Elizabeth's insistence he finally relinquished the knife to her; but only, he told her, because the blood made his fingers slippery.

When the first of the planks came away, Elizabeth let out a soft cry of pleasure. Natural light and cool fresh air . . . She had not realized how stale the air in the room was until she inhaled the real thing. Dawn was breaking over the hills. Her face pressed to the eight-inch gap, she breathed deeply.

Christian's reaction was more practical. "Damn. I'd forgotten how early the sun rises. If I hadn't wasted time bragging about how smart I am—"

"It wouldn't have mattered. At the rate we're going, it will take three or four more hours to get a second board off."

Christian was not consoled. He sank down onto his haunches, head bowed and arms limp. "We daren't risk it in daylight. Another day in this rat trap . . ."

"Why don't you get some sleep?" Elizabeth conquered the impulse to fondle his tumbled hair. "You must be exhausted."

"Might as well." He hoisted himself laboriously to his feet. "First let's replace the board. What's the schedule, or is there one?"

"They've been in here twice—except for bringing you, which was obviously a change in routine." She held the board while he tightened the screws. "I was fed both times. Lunch and dinner, presumably."

"That's encouraging. It suggests some concern for your survival." A giant yawn ended the sentence.

"Lie down," Elizabeth ordered. "You don't want them to suspect you have been awake all night. They might wonder what you were doing. If they examine the screws closely—"

"Right, right. Wait a minute."

"What is it now?"

"Tools. Get them out of sight." He gathered his pitiful little collection, together with the discarded tape, and looked around the empty room.

"Under the bed. There's no place else."

"Only too true." Christian got down and poked his head under the blanket, which hung down all the way to the floor. He sneezed. "Good. There hasn't been a mop under here for weeks."

When he pulled himself out, his hair was gray with dust. He lay still for a moment, face slack with weariness. Then he looked up at Elizabeth and remarked. "I'd offer to sleep on the couch if there was a couch."

"This is no time to be funny."

They stretched out on the bed side by side. After a while Elizabeth said, "Christian?"

"Hmmm?"

"Why is Margaret's hair green?"

"She keeps trying different hair dyes," Christian mumbled. "Last year it was purple."

"Oh. Christian? About Margaret's bathrobe—"

This time the only reply was a soft snore.

Elizabeth raised herself on one elbow and looked down at him. His mouth had relaxed, and his dusty hair and general air of dishevelment were more becoming than otherwise. She wondered if he would wake up if she kissed him. Better not risk it. He must care about her, or he wouldn't have gone to such desperate and absurd lengths to find her. Then why the devil didn't he say so? He couldn't be that insecure. Young, successful, good-looking—he must have had all the women he wanted. Maybe he didn't care. Maybe he had been driven by Duty instead of Love.

She lay down. Christian's snores increased in volume and frequency, but they did not prevent her from falling asleep, her body pressed close to his.

Her subconscious sentry was now alert to the sound of the key in the lock. She sat up with a start. Christian slept on, looking so tired and vulnerable that she was reluctant to awaken him. But she knew he would hate being roused by Schmidt's jeers, and anyway it was only a matter of seconds. She shook him. "Christian, they're coming."

He woke up instantly, awareness darkening his eyes. There was only time for an exchange of glances before the door opened.

"Sleep well?" Schmidt inquired, watching Christian try to suppress a yawn. "Or did you sleep? The more fool you if you did."

He burst into raucous laughter, delighted at his own wit. "Come on, honey. You first."

When Elizabeth returned from the bathroom, Christian was led out. Schmidt paid him the compliment of following with gun in hand, which he had not bothered to do for Elizabeth. She had hoped they would divide their strength, one guard to each prisoner, but such was not the case. Schmidt locked the door on Christian while she was out of the room and repeated the process the second time.

When Christian returned, Eric trailed him with a tray. Elizabeth sniffed expectantly as a medley of wonderful smells tickled her nostrils. Her anticipation was fully borne out by the food itself. The coffee was strong and fresh, the eggs perfectly cooked, the bread thinly sliced. The sausages were ambrosia, the best Elizabeth had ever eaten. A plate of cold ham and sliced cheese completed the repast. Since it was the first edible meal she had had in over twenty-four hours, Elizabeth may be excused for eating everything on her plate and scraping up the crumbs.

"Very good," she exclaimed, smiling at Eric. "Very, very good."

"I told you you're wasting your time on him," Schmidt said. "Anyhow, he didn't cook it."

"Oh?" She was tempted to ask if Cheryl had been pressed into service, but caution prevailed. One never knew what fragment of careless speech might be used against one.

Eric was unmoved by Elizabeth's smiles and compliments. He picked up the tray and started to leave.

"Just a minute," Christian said. "I want you to take that chain off her.

"Does it bother you?" Schmidt inquired with a grin.

"It seems excessive," Christian said in his most supercilious voice. "You haven't seen fit to confine me."

"We don't have to. You wouldn't leave without her, woule
you? Because if you did manage to get away, you might no
like what you found when you got back here with the police."

The door closed.

Elizabeth expected some comment from Christian. Instead
he sat quite still, staring fixedly at his clenched hands. Ther
he got down and crawled under the bed.

He was there for so long that Elizabeth began to get worried. She tugged at his ankle. "What are you doing?"

"Sh!" His left hand appeared from under the blanket and
made urgent gestures. "Be quiet."

Five minutes passed. She was able to measure the time
because Christian's watch was on his left wrist, which
remained in sight. Otherwise she would have sworn it was at
least an hour. She was about to tug at him again when he lev-
ered himself out.

"Nobody has moved that bed for years," he said, in a
thrilling whisper.

"I don't blame them. It must weigh two hundred pounds
Why are you so pleased about it?"

"There's a loose board. When I put my ear against the
crack I could hear what was going on downstairs."

"Anything interesting?"

He sat on the bed and pulled her down beside him. "The
room under this one is the kitchen. That seems to be wher
they spend most of their time. We were right—they are waiting to hear from Margaret."

"Really? What did they say?"

"Schmidt was grousing because they had to sit around
here doing nothing. Then the little guy—his name i
Radsky, or at least that's what Schmidt called him—Radsk
said something like 'She will contact us as soon as sh
learns her son is missing. She must. She knows what is a
stake.'"

"'Yes,'" Schmidt said, 'but it will take a while before sh
learns what has happened. We'll be stuck here for at leas
two or three more days.'"

"Two or three more days!" Elizabeth's spirits sank. "I don't think I could stand that, Christian."

"You won't have to. We'll be out of here tonight." He picked up the pocket knife and went to the window.

11

O NE OF the screws on the next board had been driven in for keeps. Christian broke the knife blade on it and had to resort to the other, longer blade, which was much thinner. It snapped on the next-to-last screw; the can opener and the bottle opener also succumbed; but before the sun had soared out of sight above the house, the second board was loose.

"I think it's wide enough," Elizabeth said, staring in disbelief. She hadn't really believed they could do it.

"It's wide enough." Cautiously Christian put his head out. "Hell and damn. Looks like a straight drop to the ground. Not even a handy vine or trellis."

"We could tear up the sheet and blanket and make a rope."

"Good idea. We—oops." He pulled his head in and slapped the boards into place. "Somebody in the yard. Here, hand me the screws."

They got them back just in time. Lunch was early that day. It was also delicious—a cheese omelet with bits of bacon and tomato and a fresh green salad. The menu testified to the inadequacy of the larder as well as the ingenuity of the cook.

Schmidt was unusually taciturn, snapping at them to hurry then slamming the door without pausing to make provocative comments.

"The delay is getting on his nerves," Christian commented. He stretched out on the bed. "I think I ate too much. This isn't such a bad place; at least the food is first-rate."

"You missed the worst of it. The first two meals were the most god-awful stew I ever tried to eat. Schmidt was complaining about it too. Somebody else must be doing the cooking."

"Nonetheless we are checking out tonight."

"Do you really think we can make it?"

"Of course." Christian's tone was a little too hearty. "That was a good idea of yours about tearing up the sheet. We had better wait till after dinner, though. They might notice."

"The waiting is going to be hard—almost harder than when I thought there wasn't a chance of escape. I wish there were something we could do to pass the time."

"I'm going to take a nap," Christian said calmly.

"Oh."

"Any objections? There's nothing we can do right now anyway."

"Why should I object? Sleep tight."

He was asleep in five minutes. Elizabeth looked down at him, her hands on her hips.

"You cold-blooded turkey," she said aloud. Christian smiled faintly and turned on his side.

Elizabeth envied him his ability to sleep. She had had ample opportunity to catch up on her own rest, and anyway she was too nervous. She yearned to look out the window but knew she ought not to take the chance. She did not want to finish *Dead Drab in a Ditch*. For lack of any other source of entertainment she dropped onto her stomach and wriggled under the bed.

It was like sliding into a heavy paper bag filled with thick, hot, dusty darkness. She found the loose board and pressed her ear to the floor.

At first she heard only a rhythmic slapping sound and an occasional murmur. Then Schmidt exclaimed, "Gin!" and she realized that the villains were whiling away the dull hours playing cards.

"That makes twenty-two bucks you owe me," Schmidt added in a pleased voice.

"So who cares?" replied a shrill voice that she recognized as Cheryl's. "We'll all be rich when this deal goes through— if you weren't putting me on."

"We'll do all right. But I wish we could wind things up. Damn that big-nosed old broad! She's really screwed us."

"You are wrong," said a soft, almost apologetic male voice. The man with the trunk and the blackjack, Elizabeth thought—Radsky. For a man so violent he sounded incredibly demure and meek.

Radsky went on, "It is not Margaret Rosenberg who is to blame but another—Eric's stupid, cowardly brother."

"He's crazy," Cheryl said. "I mean, he is really a moron, if you know what I mean."

"You mean he is mentally retarded," Radsky said. "I agree with your assessment, if not with your wording. Wolf has the intelligence of a six-year-old child."

"We shouldn't have let him in on this," Schmidt grumbled.

"We had no choice," Radsky said. "In view of the fact that he and Eric were the ones who got in touch with us. It was then a fait accompli."

"Well, but you were the one who scared him." Schmidt seemed determined to blame everyone he could. "He was all right till you started waving that knife around and telling him stories about your career."

"I had to amuse myself somehow." The little man's voice was chillingly indifferent. "He was such an appreciative audience, with his gaping mouth and his frightened eyes. Who could know that a great hulk like that would be so chicken-hearted? I could not predict he would run away."

"And contact Margaret Rosenberg. I'm surprised he had the intelligence to find her address and write it on an envelope."

"What if he's already told her where it is?" Cheryl asked.

There followed a brief silence fraught with uneasiness.

"What if he has?" Schmidt asked finally. "Once she learns we are holding her son, she won't dare—"

"But she doesn't know." Cheryl's voice rose shrilly. "I don't like this, Joe. And I don't trust that dumb ox Eric."

"He's in this as deep as we are," Schmidt said.

"No, he's not. He hasn't got a record like . . . well, like some of us. And he's goofy about his dumb brother. If he knew what you're planning to do—"

A sharp slapping sound interrupted this speech. Cheryl yelped.

"Shut up," Schmidt snapped. "He doesn't know, and he won't, if you watch your mouth."

"All right, Joe. All right. I never said nothing to him."

"Just see that you don't. Oh, hell, let's play another game. There's nothing else to do."

The slap of cards resumed.

Feeling herself on the brink of a gigantic sneeze, Elizabeth backed out of her hiding place. Christian was still asleep. She was tempted to wake him up and tell him what she had heard, but his peaceful face disarmed her, and for fear of disturbing him she settled down on the floor, her back against the side of the bed.

The conversation had confirmed a number of their theories but had not contributed much in the way of new or useful information. The silent Eric might not be a genuine member of the gang, but he was too deeply involved to be counted on for help.

Christian's suspicions about Margaret had been well founded. She had learned of—whatever it was (Margaret's bathrobe? Absurd.)—by means of a letter from Eric's brother Wolf; and Wolf could be none other than the very large person in the knitted cap who had been running on and off the stage like a character in a Pinter play. Was that why Margaret had been rambling around in what had seemed an equally aimless fashion? If her unfortunate informant was slow-witted, with a child's mind lodged in his massive body, some of his peculiar behavior was explicable. At least he had sense enough to be afraid. Perhaps he was now the only person in the world who knew the location of the mysterious object they all wanted so badly. Either he was the one who had found it in the first place, or he had taken it with him when he ran away.

As the afternoon wore on and Christian slept like a man with not a worry in the world, Elizabeth returned again and again to her listening post under the bed. The first time only silence rewarded her. Apparently her captors had left the room. Half an hour later she tried again. Still silence; she was about to withdraw when she heard a door open, and Schmidt said irritably, "Nothing yet?"

"No," was the calm reply from Radsky.

"Damn. Maybe one of us ought to go to Copenhagen."

"We were told to stay here and await news."

"Who the hell does he think he is, giving orders? You and I were doing okay till he butted in."

"He can be a valuable addition," Radsky said in the same cool voice. "And in this case he is right. We have two chances to get what we want. If Margaret Rosenberg has obtained the information from Wolf, she will give it to us in exchange for our prisoners. Our message is waiting for her at the hotel; it is the logical place for her to seek news. As for Wolf—our attempt to catch him did nothing but frighten the idiot into mindless flight. If we keep out of sight and leave him alone, he may be simple-minded enough to come home."

"A nice, neat summary," Schmidt sneered.

Elizabeth had to agree with him. Christian had been correct in his assessment of the gang's strength. There were only five of them, including the unknown "he" who was watching developments in Copenhagen.

Cheryl was the next to enter. "God, I'm bored," she announced. "How much longer do we have to stay in this hole?"

"Till the job is finished," Radsky replied. "Find something to do and stop complaining."

"There isn't anything to do. I can't go outside, and even that boring television doesn't come on till night. What a country—not even decent TV."

"Have a beer," Schmidt said. Apparently he and Cheryl had made up their differences; his tone was conciliatory.

"The beer's all gone. We're practically out of food, too. Why can't Eric go to the store?"

"I do not feel it would be wise to let Eric go off alone," Radsky said. "I am not completely convinced of his loyalty."

"Loyalty!" Cheryl laughed shrilly. "That's a good one. I wouldn't trust your loyalty to me and Joe if we stopped being useful to you." Radsky did not reply to this statement, and after a moment Cheryl went on sullenly, "When's dinner? That's the only thing to do around here—eat. If there's anything to cook."

"Well, go get the old lady and tell her we want to eat," Schmidt said. "Where is she anyhow?"

"Scrounging around in the garden. Maybe she can find some food. Looks like a lot of weeds to me."

"Damn it, she wasn't supposed to go outside!"

"She is too feeble of mind and body to constitute a danger," Radsky said. "Besides, she is a regular member of the household, and normalcy is the impression we wish to create. If I had been here when Eric sent her away, I would have told you that was a mistake."

"Anyway, she came back," Schmidt said. "A good thing, too. If I'd had to eat any more of his cooking, I'd have choked." A chair scraped across the floor, and footsteps crossed the room. "Yeah, there she is," Schmidt said. "God, what a picture—she looks like a witch, collecting her poisonous plants. Hey, old lady—yes, you. Get in here. Time for chow."

"For God's sake, Joe, she barely understands her own language, let alone English," Cheryl exclaimed. "I'll go get her."

"Don't leave the doorway," Radsky cautioned.

The bedsprings over Elizabeth's head creaked, and she slithered out. Christian was sitting up, his eyes wild as he surveyed the empty room.

"Oh, there you are," he said, as she emerged, dusty and perspiring. "Hear anything interesting?"

"Interesting but not useful." Elizabeth repeated the conversation.

Christian's first reaction was to crow about his superior insight. "I told you that letter was important. I told you Margaret had ulterior motives in coming to Denmark. I told you—"

"You told me a lot of things, most of them wrong. Nobody took a shot at you. They were shooting at Wolf that time at the Cathedral."

"Maybe so. I'm surprised they would risk killing him, though. If your ideas are right, he's the only source of the information they want."

"I suppose they were getting exasperated," Elizabeth said. "Schmidt doesn't seem to be the world's most patient man. Besides, one bullet wouldn't kill Wolf, it would just slow him down a little—and I don't know of anything else that would."

Christian dismissed this calloused assessment with a shrug. "So Eric is having second thoughts, is he? I wonder if we could make use of that."

"You mean to try to win him over to our side instead of climbing out the window? After all that work?"

"It isn't the safest exit in the world. We'll be pretty vulnerable dangling from a rope. How are you at rope climbing?"

"I've never tried it."

"I could lower you." Christian pondered. "But I had planned to be the first one down. And if something happened and one of us got busted up, we'd be in trouble"

"So what are you suggesting? There are three of them here, even without Eric."

"There are two of us."

"Gee, thanks. I guess I could handle Cheryl—if she didn't shoot me first."

"We have a knife."

"Both the blades are broken."

Christian refused to be discouraged. "There's a file on the pocket knife. Suppose I sharpen the picklock?"

"Could you really stick that into somebody's back?" Elizabeth demanded.

"Into Schmidt's I could," was the unhesitating reply. "If we unscrew the lightbulb, the room will be totally dark. As soon as he came in I could stab him."

"And I could persuade Eric to join the good guys," Elizabeth said. "Which wouldn't be too easy even if I could speak Danish. In the meantime Radsky would come up the stairs with his blackjack in one hand and his gun in the other."

"No, no. You hide behind the door and hit Eric over the head. We haven't time for debate."

"What do I hit him with?"

"The chain," Christian said triumphantly. "It's heavy. As you ought to know."

"Speaking of the chain," Elizabeth said, overcome by a horrible qualm.

"No problem. That's where my handy picklock comes in."

"If you sharpen the picklock into a knife, you can't use it to pick a lock," said Elizabeth, leaving unvoiced her suspicion that this latter activity might not be as easy as Christian believed. "Oh, this is ridiculous! Control your bloodthirsty impulses and face reality. We're much better off with the window. Speaking of which, don't you think maybe we ought to start working on the chain?"

"No, I don't. Eric opens and closes the lock when he takes you downstairs. We don't want any signs of tampering."

"Then there's nothing we can do until after they bring our dinner."

"No." Christian closed his eyes.

"Are you going to sleep *again?*"

"Any other ideas?"

"Well, we could eavesdrop some more. They might say something important."

Christian assented graciously to this suggestion. It was necessary for them to put their heads close together, and Elizabeth found the position extremely distracting. Christian's warm breath tickled her chin. Then she started convulsively as a high, shrill keening sound pierced her ear.

"What the hell is she doing that for?" Schmidt's voice asked.

"I believe she is singing," said Radsky, amused.

"It's the most god-awful noise I ever heard. Hey, Grandma, cut that out."

"Leave her alone," Cheryl said. "She's not hurting anything."

The keening rose to a pitch that made Elizabeth want to clap her hand over her ear. "Jee-sus," Schmidt shouted. "So help me, Grannie, if you don't stop that—"

"She does not understand you," Radsky said. "The woman is senile, I tell you. But if that unearthly noise assists her culinary skills, then okay."

"It smells good," Cheryl said.

"The food is all right; it's the floor show I can't stand," muttered Schmidt.

Elizabeth had to agree with him. The shrill voice had an eerie, monotonous persistence that reminded her of Satanists summoning up demons.

"Go in the other room, then," Cheryl said. "You better check on Eric anyhow. I can't see him from the window."

Schmidt retreated, slamming the kitchen door.

Christian was the next to surrender. Murmuring, "I think I'm going deaf," he pulled himself out. Elizabeth remained doggedly at her post until a great clashing of pan lids was followed by Radsky's question, "Is it ready, Mother? Good."

Elizabeth decided it was time to come out. "They'll probably be up here pretty soon," she reported, peering over the edge of the bed at Christian, who was lying down, hands clasped under his head.

"The sooner the better," was the reply.

Even if she had not overheard evidence of Schmidt's increasing ill temper, Elizabeth would have sensed the change in the atmosphere as soon as he appeared. He was holding his gun in plain sight, and he behaved as if he wanted an excuse to use it. His inquiries as to how they had whiled away the afternoon hours were loaded with unsubtle and offensive innuendos, and he kept watching Christian with a greedy, anticipatory smirk. Elizabeth felt sure he was wasting his time. Christian was too cool and level-headed to be provoked into a reckless move; but he was unquestionably the one Schmidt was after. When Schmidt escorted Elizabeth downstairs he didn't even speak to her, except for a curt, "Don't take all day." When Christian returned, Elizabeth could tell by his flushed face and tight lips that Schmidt had been needling him.

After Eric had placed the tray on the bed, Schmidt motioned him to leave. The big man would have protested, but Schmidt used the hand that held the gun to repeat his gesture of dismissal, and Eric plodded out.

"Come here, sweetheart," Schmidt said.

"Who, me?" Elizabeth asked.

"I'm not talking to lover boy. Come here."

Elizabeth was not afraid for herself. Schmidt was interested in violence, not sex. He was bored and tense, and like all persons of limited imagination, the only thing he could think of was to hit someone. Elizabeth considered screaming for help. Radsky impressed her as more practical than his ally; he wouldn't want to risk damaging his hostages.

Before she could decide what to do, Schmidt started moving toward her.

"Leave her alone," Christian said.

Schmidt laughed and made a lunge for Elizabeth. He caught her wrist and pulled on it, dragging her to her knees.

Christian hit him. It was a neat, clean uppercut to the jaw, and it was probably the most ineffectual of all possible blows. It staggered Schmidt but did not seriously inconvenience him. With a little grunt of satisfaction he reversed the gun and swung it in a sweeping arc aimed at Christian's face. Christian saw it coming and tried to pull back. The movement gained him a vital half inch and probably saved him from a fractured jaw, but the blow was hard enough to topple him. He hit the floor with a crash and lay still.

Schmidt's smile had the sleepy, sated look of someone who has just relieved a pressing need. He shook himself and slipped the gun into his pocket.

"See you later, sweetheart," he said, and went out.

Elizabeth got down on her knees beside Christian. His eyes were open. One hand nursed his bleeding cheek.

"Christian!" Elizabeth cried. She raised his head in her arms. "Oh, Christian, darling!"

"Oh, God," said Christian.

"That was not a smart thing to do," Elizabeth said.

Christian freed himself from her embrace and sat up, supporting his back against the bed. He glared at her for a moment, his lips moving, as if he were searching for a devastating retort. Words failed him. Grabbing her by the shoulders, he pulled her across his lap and kissed her till her ears started to ring.

It was Christian who finally stopped things. Conspicuously short of breath, he remarked, "I think this is turning into a different type of movie."

"Don't be a pedant."

He captured her hand and brought it to his lips—an unexpected gesture that would have destroyed her remaining defenses if they had not already lain in ruins.

"I love you," she said.

"I love you, too, and in the near future I hope to demonstrate it at length. Right now I'm too preoccupied with other problems to do either of us justice."

Gently Elizabeth touched his bleeding cheek. "Does it hurt?"

"Yes, it hurts. What an idiotic question. No thanks to me that it isn't worse. I shouldn't have let him get to me."

"Stop blaming yourself. If you hadn't hit him, I would have."

"Don't think he doesn't know that. I just hope to God he doesn't get uptight again and come back for another round."

"Let's get started, then. The sooner we're out of here, the better."

Christian retrieved the broken knife blade from under the bed and handed it to her. "See what you can do with the sheet while I work on the chain."

The single sheet was heavy old linen, coarse and stiff. Without the knife Elizabeth would have had a hard time tearing it. When she had finally braided it into a strand that looked stout enough to bear Christian's weight, it made a depressingly short rope.

"We'll have to use the blanket too," she reported. "How are you coming?"

Christian's manipulations with the picklock had been accompanied by grunts and curses. "I'll get it," he replied, without looking up.

"Maybe we could lift the bed and unwind it," Elizabeth suggested.

"You can't go running around the countryside with twenty pounds of chain draped over your arm," was the querulous reply. "And lifting the bed wouldn't be enough. I'd have to take it apart. Ow. Damn!"

The picklock had slipped again. Elizabeth should have been depressed by the confirmation of what she had feared— that picking a lock was a skill possible only to trained experts. But her mood was incorrigibly exhilarated. She refused to admit the possibility that her love affair would begin and end in this horrible little room. Tactfully she refrained from further comments and reached for the blanket.

In order to remove it from the bed she had to shift the tray, which she had forgotten—as, apparently, had Schmidt. When she gave it a closer look she understood why he had not been concerned. There were no plates or utensils or bottles on it, only a pile of sandwiches and a plastic container of water. The tray itself was wood, too flimsy to serve as a bludgeon.

"They ate it all up," she remarked, lifting the tray and pulling the blanket from under it.

"What?"

"The lovely meal the singing cook prepared. They must have eaten every scrap. All we got was ham sandwiches."

Christian did not reply. His breathing consisted almost entirely of muttered expletives.

Dismembering the blanket was a much more difficult job than tearing the sheet. It was wool, hardened by innumerable washings into a consistency resembling felt. Elizabeth's hands were sore before she had it in pieces, but when she finished fastening the strips together, the length looked promising. She watched Christian's increasingly frenzied efforts for a few moments before she spoke.

"If worse comes to worst, you'll have to go for help."

"No."

"They won't come in here before morning. You'll have plenty of time."

"No."

His hands were bleeding from dozens of tiny cuts where the tool had slipped. Elizabeth's throat tightened. She had to clear it before she spoke.

"Give it a rest. It's early yet. Why don't you eat something?"

She thought Christian was going to hurl the infuriating instrument across the room, but he controlled himself. "Okay," he said. "That's a good idea."

She knew what was driving him because the same fear made her heart beat too fast. Schmidt was frighteningly unpredictable in his present mood. There was no guarantee

that the familiar routine would be followed. She understood
the effort it cost Christian to stop working and felt the sickness that surged up in him when he bit into food that was an
affront to his churning stomach.

"It's very good ham," she said, chewing valiantly.

"Naturally. Denmark is famous for—" He let out a howl,
dropped the sandwich, and clapped his hand to his jaw.

"What on earth—"

"I just about broke a tooth," Christian said indistinctly.
"Some ass left a piece of bone or—" But the object he
extracted from the uneaten interior of the sandwich was not
bone. It gleamed in the light.

"It's a key," Elizabeth gasped. "Oh, Christian, do you
think . . . "

"It's too small to be the key to the door." Slowly, almost
fearfully, as if frustration of this new hope would be too
much to bear, he tried the key in the lock of the iron anklet.
The click was the sweetest sound Elizabeth had ever heard.

"I don't believe it," Christian muttered. His fingers
caressed her ankle. "I never did believe in literal responses to
prayer."

"With all due respect to God, I think it's Eric we have to
thank for this miracle."

"Right. It must have been Eric."

"I wonder why he brought the key tonight, of all nights."

"He's not as slow as he looks," Christian said. "Maybe he
noticed we've been working on the window. I'll bet he's the
one who put the boards up; Schmidt and Radsky aren't
handyman types. Or else—maybe he's received word that
Wolf is in the neighborhood. He knows what will happen to
the poor devil if that bunch get their hands on him, and they
have made sure he has no way of warning his brother."

At least the weather was on their side; as usual, the skies
were gloomy, and rain appeared imminent. Even so, night
crept on with maddeningly coy deliberation. The delay was
doubly agonizing because it involved a choice on their part.
The later the hour, the better their chances of escape, but

there was the ever-present danger that someone would come
upstairs. A single glance would betray their plans.

Christian summarized the situation. "If anyone comes up
those stairs, we go out the window. It's that simple."

They did all they could do to minimize the risk. The
boards were loose, held by a few threads of screw; a single
wrench would remove them. The makeshift rope was fas-
tened to the bedpost. Christian stood by the window peering
out through a crack. Elizabeth was under the bed listening.
From time to time they changed places.

The members of the gang were in the kitchen, but there
was not much conversation. The amplitude of the evening
meal had reduced them to satisfied silence and—in
Schmidt's case—belches. From the fact that no one made a
remark about him or his missing brother, Elizabeth deduced
that Eric was present, and typically taciturn.

Some time later Schmidt said abruptly. "Think I'll have a
look at our little birds in their cage."

Elizabeth came as close to a heart attack as she would
come for another thirty years. Before she could move
Radsky said, "No, you will not. There is too much at stake
for your games. You lack control."

Schmidt grumbled, but did not insist.

She mentioned this exchange to Christian when they
changed places, thinking it would reassure him. It only made
him angry, and there was a hopeful light in his eyes when he
said, "I almost wish the son of a bitch would come up."

A few hours earlier this would have prompted Elizabeth to
a sarcastic reference to his wounds and bruises. Now she
said, "You can beat him up later, darling. I promise," and
stood on tiptoe to brush his cheek with her lips.

"Thanks," Christian said, grinning. He disappeared under
the bed.

Elizabeth took up her post at the window. The night air
was cool and damp. The lighted square of the kitchen window cast an increasingly distinct outline on the ground below
and to her left. If their luck held—if Radsky could contro

Schmidt—then when that square of light disappeared, signaling bedtime, their chances of escape would be multiplied several times over. But how slowly darkness crept in! She felt as if she had aged ten years for every minute that passed.

Sounds carried distinctly on the still air. The infrequent, distant rush of a car passing on the road was a reminder that freedom lay only a short distance away. The only other noise was the rustle of foliage. Once, far off in the distance, she heard a wolflike howling that made her skin prickle until she realized it was probably only a neighbor's dog.

Then her skin prickled again, in earnest, as she remembered Christian's nemesis. It was no wonder she had forgotten the dog; she had not heard it or even any reference to it. It must be a remarkably silent animal. It had not been silent, though, when Christian tried to pass she shed where it was confined. She wondered whether Christian had also forgotten this danger or whether he had simply decided they must deal with it when and if it arose.

During her next stint under the bed she heard Cheryl announce that she was going to bed. One down, Elizabeth thought—two to go. Surely Eric could be counted out as an adversary. The gift of the key proved he wished them success, even if he was unable or unwilling to take more positive action.

She hoped Schmidt would follow Cheryl, but apparently the card game was going well for him. He and Radsky continued to play, and they were still at it when she changed places with Christian.

When she looked out the window, darkness was almost complete. If they had to make a run for it now, they would have a good chance of being unseen. She was exhausted with strain; she actually began to nod as she stared, half hypnotized, at the square of light that represented the last impalpable barrier between them and their attempt to escape. Prison bars of light, walls of illumination . . .

Then she heard a sound that woke her completely and caused her to press her face to the crack between the boards.

The sound continued and increased in volume—the crunch
ing of gravel and the rustling of branches being moved aside
Someone was coming. Someone whose heavy breathing was
occasionally interrupted by snuffling sobs.

The dog could not have heard this pathetic expression of
woe. As Elizabeth learned later, the animal was kept in a
windowless shed on the other side of the farmhouse. What
sense it was that alerted it she never knew—perhaps the sixth
sense that exists between animals and their masters. The sud
den outburst of barks and whines and yelps was an expres
sion of joyous greeting, not a watchdog's alarm.

The newcomer was now visible as a large dark shape on
the graveled driveway. It responded with a whimper that
sounded like an echo of the dog's, and blundered off behind
the house.

Christian came shooting out from under the bed as Eliza
beth turned from the window. "It's Wolf," they exclaimed
simultaneously. Christian jumped onto the bed, spit inele
gantly onto his fingers, and unscrewed the light bulb
Darkness fell like a muffling cloak.

Elizabeth had the first board off the window when
Christian joined her. Together they removed the second
board. She expected to hear shouts and the sounds of a fran
tic pursuit, but only the rapturous whines of the dog met her
ears. Then she understood. They would creep up on the
unsuspecting innocent while he was greeting his pet. Either
he had been watching the house and had concluded there was
no danger, or else loneliness and fear had driven him back to
the only safety he had ever known.

Christian looped one end of the rope under Elizabeth's
arms.

"Shouldn't we wait?" she whispered. "They're all out
there, hunting him—"

"They'll be too busy to notice us. Besides, what if they
decide to bring him up here? Quick!"

They had planned the procedure in detail, and it went as
neatly as if they had actually rehearsed it. The descent was

over before Elizabeth had time to wonder whether it would work. She moved out of the way as Christian slid down to stand beside her. There were two rectangles of light on the ground now. The kitchen door stood wide open.

They shrank back into the scanty concealment offered by the open door and some straggling bushes as a small procession came into sight around the corner of the house. Schmidt and Radsky each held one of Wolf's huge ankles; their combined strength was barely enough to drag him. His cap had fallen off and his head bumped along the ground. As the movers paused for breath in the light from the kitchen window, Elizabeth saw that the big man's face was stained with blood. He was alive, though. His broad chest heaved up and down like a bellows.

"Hurry," Radsky grunted. "We must confine him before he wakes."

"I wish I'd shot him," Schmidt said, wiping his forehead with his shirt sleeve. "That would slow him down."

"More likely it would send him into a berserk rage. Hurry, I tell you. I have never dealt with a skull so thick; I cannot calculate how long he will be unconscious."

The two bent to their task again. Grunting and gasping, they inched the enormous body through the door. Wolf's head banged on the sill as they heaved the last part of him inside. Except for the blood on his face he might have been peacefully sleeping.

For a perilous moment the escapees stood motionless, Christian's arms holding Elizabeth tightly. She knew what kept him from moving, for she felt the same; she hated to leave the big, harmless man to the tender mercies of Schmidt and Radsky. But what could they do, without a weapon?

Slowly they moved away from the door, which was still open. Christian took the lead, holding Elizabeth's hand. He knew the terrain and she did not; she was content to let him guide her, though she sensed they were moving away from the road, which would seem to be the quickest route to rescue. But if they had gone directly toward it they would have had to pass the open kitchen door; and perhaps after all it would be wiser to seek concealment in the woods. If their escape was discovered, the pursuers would assume they were heading for the highway.

Their route led them among the outbuildings of the farm, including the shed in which the dog was kept. The animal was still whining and whimpering, bewildered by the disappearance of its master. The whines changed to barks as the fugitives neared the shed, but it was not the dog that betrayed their escape. One of the gang must have gone upstairs. They were close enough to the house to hear a bellow of fury from Schmidt: "They're gone! Quick, after them."

"The lights, you fool," Radsky shouted back.

"Head for the woods," Christian said in his normal voice. There was no need to whisper; between the barking and the uproar from the house, nothing softer than a scream could have been heard. But they were still in the farmyard when they learned the meaning of Radsky's enigmatic order. Suddenly the whole area was illuminated by a harsh white glare. Eric had installed floodlights on the back of the house and the outbuildings.

For a moment the fugitives were blinded. It was immediately apparent the their pursuers had not been so affected. A bullet whizzed past Elizabeth and struck a post with a thunking sound.

Instinctively they both fell flat. To the now frantic howls of the dog had been added another equally frenzied sound, like the bellowing of a herd of elephants. Elizabeth had no time to speculate on the source of the noise—she didn't really believe it could be elephants—but she hoped the maddened creatures were safely penned up.

A second bullet chunked into the fence. No sound of an explosion accompanied it; Radsky was apparently using a silencer. Raising her head a scant inch, Elizabeth saw that the fence enclosed them on two sides, with a solid wooden barrier, part of a building, barring escape on the third side. The

fourth, open side faced the house, and the guns of their pursuers.

"This way," Christian muttered. He started to crawl
toward the only possible way out—a door in the wooden
wall.

As they neared the door Elizabeth became aware of a
strange and horrible odor. It was the concentrated essence—
perhaps the origin—of the smell she had noticed on Eric's
clothes. Not only did the odor increase in strength as they
crawled toward the building, but so did the ghastly cacopho-
ny that formed a counterpoint to the dog's barking. It held a
note of almost human frenzy.

Christian had to rise to his knees to lift the metal latch that
held the door. He pulled his hand back in a hurry when a bullet struck the wood and sent splinters flying. But the door
was now ajar, and without wasting time in gallantry Christian slid through the opening. A veritable fog of foul odor
oozed out of the crack. Had it not been for Christian's vigorously gesturing hand and the vivid memory of the bullet that
had narrowly missed that hand, Elizabeth would have preferred to remain outside. Never had she encountered a stench
to equal the one that assaulted her nostrils, and she dared not
imagine what monstrosity was capable of producing it.

Christian yanked her in and closed the door. Darkness,
stench, and howling enveloped them. It was the lesser of two
evils, but just barely. Elizabeth clutched Christian in un-
shamed terror. "It's horrible—horrible! Oh, what is it?"

The darkness heaved with the movement of slow, ponderous bodies. "Pigs," Christian said, surprised. "It's a pig farm.
Didn't you know?"

He switched on the tiny flashlight and moved it around,
giving Elizabeth a long-drawn-out but adequate view of the
interior of the place.

It was of considerable size, with pens on either side and a
mucky, muddy path running down the center. The pens were
inhabited by pigs of all sizes, ranging from enormous pork-

ers to tiny piglets hardly longer than her hand. Most of them
were white. Elizabeth giggled self-consciously.

"I never knew they smelled so bad."

"They may smell, but they are very intelligent. Hey, watch
out." He caught her hand as she reached out to pat the near-
est pig. They were so much less offensive than Schmidt and
Radsky—in everything except smell—that she felt quite
affectionate toward them.

"The big boars can be mean," Christian warned. "And
there is nothing nastier than a sow with piglets. They weigh
as much as four hundred pounds."

"This is no time to discuss pigs," Elizabeth said hysterically. "We're trapped. What are we going to do?"

"Whatever we do will have to be done fast. They know
we're in here and they know we're unarmed. They can simply walk in and—"

A shout interrupted him. It sounded as if the speaker were
just outside the door.

"Come out with your hands up, Rosenberg."

"Play for time," Elizabeth said.

"Time isn't going to do us any good." But he replied, in a
shout that set the pigs to squealing nervously, "Why should
we come out?"

"Because if you do not, we will shoot to kill." This reply
came from behind them. Christian spun around with a muttered curse, switching off the light. The voice had been
Radsky's. He was at one of the windows at the far end.

"We will kill you rather than let you escape," Radsky continued. "But if you give yourself up you have nothing to fear
but a few more hours of imprisonment."

"I don't believe you."

"Then you are not being logical. We are practical men. We
do not risk a charge of murder without reason. Once we have
what we want, we will leave you in peace."

"Give me time to think it over," Christian answered.

"Five minutes. We are a trifle pressed."

"I'll bet," Elizabeth said bitterly. "They can hardly wait to get back in there and start torturing Wolf. Radsky is lying, Christian. It's a trick."

"Maybe."

"How can you doubt it?"

"They have Wolf. He'll give them the information they want . . . one way or another. I know," he went on, as Elizabeth made a soft, protesting sound. "I know it sounds callous. But Wolf is in for it, no matter what we do. We can't help him. I'm inclined to believe Radsky because his reasoning is eminently practical and totally selfish. These people probably have criminal records, but their crimes may not include murder. Professional thieves and con men try to avoid that. It isn't as if we were the only ones who could identify them. Roger and Marie, Margaret, the witnesses at the airport . . ."

They had moved together in the darkness and stood with their arms around one another. "Then you think we should just give up?" Elizabeth asked.

"Hell, no. I'm simply pointing out that if the brilliant scheme I am about to put into effect fails, we won't be any worse off than we were before. So cheer up."

Before she could answer, he had scooped her up in his arms and lifted her over one of the low wooden partitions that defined the pens. "I'll be right with you," he said. "Don't move."

A warm, bristly surface brushed Elizabeth's leg. Her yelp blended with the chorus of squeals that broke out all around her. Before she could obey her first impulse—to climb over the partition—Christian considerately turned on the flashlight and gave her a quick view of her surroundings. She was sharing the pen of three round fat white pigs, obviously triplets, and obviously only a few months old. At the sight of her they rushed forward, squeaking a demand for food, or possibly affection. She backed into a corner of the pen and stood at bay while three wet snouts nuzzled her calves.

Christian moved to the door.

"Time's up," Schmidt shouted.

"Come and get me," Christian called back, adding an uncomplimentary epithet.

He retreated, pausing briefly at each pen. The pigs were already agitated; it required little persuasion to arouse in them a restless wanderlust. Christian jumped over the partition into the pen with Elizabeth and the Three Little Pigs just in time to avoid the rush of an immense sow who charged him, her multiple udders swinging.

When Schmidt kicked the door open, the avalanche of round white bodies bowled him clean over. A flood of pork poured out the opening.

"Now!" Christian lifted Elizabeth over the partition. They followed the porcine torrent, finding the path clear except for one minuscule piglet that had fallen behind in its pursuit of mama.

The yard was more encumbered. Most of the pigs were bewildered by the lights and the unexpected freedom. They were milling aimlessly and grunting in a nervous fashion. Schmidt was rolled up like an embryo, knees under his chin, both arms covering his head. A medium-sized pig was nibbling at his hair.

Christian's face was distorted with wild amusement. He vaulted a pig with agile grace and reached for Elizabeth's hand.

The bullet hit the ground just ahead of them, sending up a spout of mud like a miniature geyser. This time they heard the shot.

Sheer momentum carried them on a few feet, but they both knew it was hopeless. Radsky had given them one last warning; the next shot wouldn't be aimed at the ground. In the glaring light he could hardly miss.

"Very sensible," Radsky said approvingly, as they came to a stop. "Now turn, both of you."

He stood by the fence, his feet apart and both hands grasping the weapon. Out of the corner of her eye Elizabeth saw

Schmidt uncurl himself and stand up. He started walking toward them.

"Stay out of the line of fire, you fool," Radsky said sharply.

Schmidt kept coming. He looked like a sleepwalker, eyes glazed, bared front teeth gleaming like fangs. The right side of his body was coated with damp earth, and a distinct odor of pig accompanied him. He paid no attention to the animals that wandered across his path. His eyes were fixed, unblinkingly, on Christian.

"If you put him to sleep, you'll have to carry him yourself," Radsky said coolly, "I've had enough of that activity lately."

12

TIED HAND and foot to stout kitchen chairs, which were in turn lashed to the supports of a tall built-in cupboard, Elizabeth and Christian contemplated each other dispiritedly. Christian was gagged as well as bound. At the last minute Schmidt had decided to let him walk into the house on his own two feet, but once his hands were tied, Schmidt had hit him a few times, and Christian had resorted to verbal abuse, having no other means of retaliation available. Tiring of his comments, Schmidt had stuffed a dishcloth into his mouth.

Elizabeth was not inclined toward conversation anyway. She could only pray that Radsky had meant what he said, and hope that Christian wouldn't strangle with suppressed fury. One of Schmidt's slaps had reopened the gash on his cheek, and the bloodstained gag was a fearsome sight. His hair was standing up in agitated tufts and his eyes bulged with opinions he was unable to express. And this was the man whom she had once despised as cold-blooded and conventional!

On the whole, Elizabeth preferred to fix her eyes on his beloved if battered countenance rather than watch what was going on elsewhere in the room. The unfortunate Wolf had been so swathed in ropes, towels, and other bonds that very little of his clothing was visible between them, and the interrogation was about to begin. Eric was nowhere in sight. Elizabeth assumed he was imprisoned somewhere, and she understood Schmidt's ruffled and unkempt appearance. He had had a busy night, overcoming Eric, dragging Wolf, and being trampled by pigs.

Cheryl had pulled up a chair and was watching interestedly while Radsky made his preparations to persuade Wolf. They were not complex—only the detailed inspection and polishing of a long, thin knife, which he had taken from a leather scabbard strapped to his side. The lights dazzled off the blade as he turned it. Wolf let out a whimper.

"He recognizes it," Radsky said coolly. "I told him tales about it. . . . Now, my very large and simple-minded friend, I hope your feeble brain has not forgotten where you put Margaret's bathrobe."

Elizabeth exchanged a startled look with her necessarily silent associate. So the seemingly insane phrase did have meaning. It meant something to Wolf. Tears began to roll down his vast cheeks, forming puddles on either side of his head.

Radsky walked slowly toward him, brandishing the knife. "Speak to him," he ordered Cheryl. "Tell him we must know where it is."

Cheryl addressed the big man in halting Danish. His head turned toward her when she spoke, but instead of replying he sobbed harder.

"I can't stand this," Elizabeth muttered. Christian tugged vainly at the ropes, then subsided, beads of perspiration standing out on his forehead. Cheryl repeated the question. She had to shout to make herself heard over Wolf's wails. From the hall beyond the open kitchen door, two more instruments added themselves to the orchestrated din—a violent rattling and banging and a high keening voice, rising and falling in an eerie chant.

Schmidt jumped up. "I'll shut the old witch up! What the hell is she saying?"

Cheryl listened, and then reported, "She keeps yelling, 'Tell them what they want to know, tell them what they want to know.'"

"And very good advice, too," said Radsky. "Do you hear, Wolf?"

Wolf wept louder, the imprisoned cook kept shrieking, and the banging increased in volume. Schmidt started for the door. He looked extremely rattled.

"Stay here," Radsky ordered. "Why do you let a helpless old woman get on your nerves?"

"If she's the one kicking the door, she's not so helpless," Schmidt muttered. "Holy God!"

"That's Eric," Cheryl said. "In the basement. He must of heard me when I yelled at Wolf."

"The whole goddamn neighborhood can hear you," Schmidt bellowed.

"Shut up!" Radsky brought the knife down in a whistling arc. The gesture silenced Schmidt and Cheryl. Even Wolf stopped weeping and stared at Radsky with mute terror.

In the silence the cries of the elderly prisoner wavered up and down the scale like a Buddhist anthem. Eric's kicks on the door had developed a regular rhythm, and Elizabeth's head began to nod in time. She had never realized that incipient tragedy could have overtones of pure slapstick. The old lady's howls and the steady banging reminded her of some of the rock groups she had heard.

Radsky was beginning to show signs of strain, and from the uneasy way in which his colleagues eyed him, Elizabeth realized that this was a bad omen. Radsky was dangerous enough when he kept his temper. She hated to think what he was like when he lost it.

With an effort that reddened his pale face, the little man controlled himself and returned to the matter at hand. Wolf watched him like a rabbit hypnotized by the baleful stare of a snake.

"Now, Wolf, you must tell me," he said softly. He knelt on the floor by his prisoner. Elizabeth closed her eyes.

She need not have worried. Wolf began to talk in a frantic high-pitched flow of words, interrupted occasionally by gurgles as tears ran into his mouth.

"First he says nothing, then he will not stop," Radsky complained. "What the devil is he saying?"

"I think he's trying to tell us where it is," Cheryl said uncertainly.

"That is very good news. *What is he saying?*"

"I can't understand!" Cheryl's voice also rose. "He talks funny. He always did talk funny, and now he's so scared he's not making any sense. Don't you yell at me, Radsky!"

Elizabeth opened her eyes. Radsky had risen to his feet. Wolf continued to talk, but whether he was confessing, begging for mercy, or simply making conversation none of them ever knew. Radsky walked up and down the room a few times. The exercise seemed to calm him; his angry color subsided, and after another turn or two he said, "We must get Eric to talk to him."

"First sensible suggestion you've made," Schmidt growled. "I'll go get him."

He vanished into the hall. A door opened. The keening rose intolerably and then stopped, with a croak.

"Get out of there," Radsky shouted. "I told you to leave her alone."

"All right, all right," Schmidt yelled back. "She was driving me crazy."

He slammed the door, and for a few seconds there was blessed silence. Elizabeth realized that for the past five minutes everyone had been screaming.

Schmidt returned with Eric. The farmer's face was as wooden as ever, but when he saw the roped bundle on the floor, agonized life flooded into it. Ignoring Schmidt's gun, he dropped to his knees beside Wolf. The latter's enormous face opened in a pleased smile. He said something to Eric, who looked at Schmidt.

"Please—don't hurt. He will tell. Please."

"Well, thank God," Schmidt said. "Talk to him, Eric."

The sight of his brother had restored Wolf's confidence. He chatted cheerfully in a sweet, high-pitched voice that sounded odd coming from his huge throat. But his eyes kept wandering uneasily to Radsky, who held the knife in plain view.

"He tells," Eric said finally. "It is in the tomb, the . . . What is the word—I do not know the English. . . . "

Radsky's face darkened. "I do not allow jokes," he snapped, flourishing the knife. Wolf let out a howl.

"You are cruel men," Eric said gravely. "I did not know. Now, too late. I tell. I try to tell. In the tomb, the very old tomb. Where the Viking chief was long ago."

"What the hell is he talking about?" Cheryl demanded. "He's stalling, Radsky. Show him—"

"No." Radsky stroked his chin. "I think I know what he means. Eric—draw a map."

"Yes." Eric got to his feet. "Then you go. Not hurt . . . " His gesture included Elizabeth and Christian, a kindly thought that she appreciated.

"Yes, yes. I give you my word."

A strange expression that might have been irony crossed Eric's face. "You lie," he said carefully, "I kill."

"*You* lie, *I* kill," Radsky retorted. "Make the map. We go to see. If you lie—we come back."

The farmer nodded. He and Radsky went to the table on the far side of the room and bent over a sheet of paper. From time to time Eric spoke briefly in Danish, referring to the map he was drawing. Radsky seemed to understand. Finally he picked up the paper. "Done," he said.

"I can't believe it," Cheryl exclaimed. "Wow, will it be great to get out of this hole!"

"Get your things," Radsky ordered. "Schmidt—"

"Yeah, I know." Schmidt gestured to Eric. "Back in the cellar, pal."

Eric turned to Radsky. "You not come back?"

"If we find it where Wolf says it is."

"It is there." Eric spoke gently to his brother. Wolf nodded agreeably, and Schmidt escorted Eric out of the room.

Radsky studied his knife with the disappointed look of a violinist who has expected to perform but has not been asked. Carefully he sheathed it. Then he looked at Christian.

"You are an impetuous young man," he said. "Do not yield to that weakness now. Only hope that the imbecile remembered correctly and that his brother interpreted accurately. If we find what we seek, we will not see you again."

"You'll find it." Elizabeth spoke with more confidence than she had reason to feel. "But you can't leave us here like this!"

"The farmer will get out of the cellar eventually," was the disinterested reply. "The door is stout and will resist for a time; but he will get out. That is why I advise you to save your strength. You will be here for a while."

Schmidt came back with Cheryl. Each carried a suitcase. "Let's go," Schmidt said.

"Start the car. I will get my bag and meet you at the front door." Radsky went out without looking at the captives. Schmidt gave them one of his vulpine smiles.

"See you around, sweetheart," he said. "You too, bright boy." He took a step toward Christian, who glared at him speechlessly.

"You leave him alone," Elizabeth shouted. Apparently the invisible crooner in the room down the hall heard her; the shrill wailing started up again. Schmidt swore, Elizabeth laughed, and Cheryl stamped her foot like a pettish school-girl. "For God's sake, Joe, let's get out of here!"

Like Cheryl—and it was the first time she had shared an emotion with that unpleasant young woman—Elizabeth could hardly believe it was over. She strained her ears to hear the sounds that meant deliverance—doors slamming, a car's engine starting up and growing softer as the vehicle moved away.

Scarcely had it died into silence when a door opened, with such vehemence that it slammed into the wall.

Footsteps pounded along the hall, and in the doorwa
appeared an apparition so bizzare that it took Elizabeth
breath away.

The word "eldritch" means weird, eerie, uncanny.
implies a wealth of richer images—the three witches on th
desolate heath prophesying to Macbeth; the wicked queen
"Snow White," hideously transformed into a horrible o
hag. The word and all its connotations were scarcely ad
quate to describe the old woman who stood before the
Tattered locks of gray hair, coarse as hemp, half conceal
her face. Steel-rimmed glasses, mended with tape at the te
ples, reflected the light like the multifaceted eyes of an en
mous insect. Her nose was so long and her chin so protru
ing that the two almost met.

The glasses flashed as she surveyed the room, one ha
stroking her chin. It came off in her hand. She threw
absently over her shoulder.

The nose stood out in all its Roman splendor, a crag j
ting out of a field of uncut hay.

II

Wolf giggled and spoke in a high, amused voice. Marga
replied; but her attention was concentrated on her son, wh
eyes threatened to pop out of his head.

"Oh, my poor darling! What have they done to you?"

She removed the gag and mopped his face with it, maki
the smeared mess even worse. "Darling, we haven't time
talk," she went on, cutting off Christian's attempt to spe
"We must hurry. Perhaps we can get there before they d
think we can. My poor sweet boy, all that blood . . . May
you had better stay here. Elizabeth and I will go af
Margaret's bathrobe. I'm sorry to trouble you, Elizabeth,
if you don't mind . . ."

Elizabeth had recovered her breath, but speech was s
beyond her. She nodded dumbly.

"Mother," Christian said. "Will you please stop patting me and untie my hands?"

"A knife would be quicker," Margaret said. She reached for one of the knives that filled a rack above the sink. It had a twelve-inch blade, and at the sight of it Christian expostulated vehemently.

"Oh, no, you don't. I've seen you trying to carve a roast. I know you're going to cut me, but at least use a smaller knife."

"Perhaps you are right," Margaret said humbly. She selected a paring knife and disappeared behind Christian. A look of mingled apprehension and resignation settled on his face.

"Were you the one who put the key in the sandwiches?" he inquired, flinching.

"No, dear, that was Eric. I suggested it, though. Oh, I'm so sorry. Did I—?"

"Never mind, get on with it."

"The ropes are very tight," Margaret complained. "The key? Yes, I thought it might be useful. You dealt with the boarded-up window very nicely; Eric saw it immediately, but did not believe Mr. Schmidt noticed. He felt, however, that you might have some trouble with Elizabeth's—er—ankle cuff. Oh, I've cut you again. Forgive me, dear."

"Keep talking," Christian said between his teeth. "You expected us to escape tonight?"

"Well, I certainly hoped you would. And you'd have done it too, clever man, if it hadn't been for Wolf." Hearing his name, the big man chuckled and spoke, Margaret tossed back a quick, smiling sentence before continuing. "It wasn't his fault, poor thing. When he was unable to locate me, he couldn't think where else to go."

"I won't ask how you knew we were here," Christian said. "You had known Eric and Wolf before?"

"Of course, they are old friends. That is why Wolf got in touch with me. And I knew Eric must be involved, if Wolf was. Honestly, Christian, I couldn't tell you about it. Though

Wolf's letter was somewhat incoherent, it was plain that the
had committed . . . well, let us call it a slight legal indiscre
tion. I hoped I could persuade the authorities to drop th
charges if the bathrobe was returned."

"What in heaven's name is—" Elizabeth began.

"Later, Elizabeth," Christian interrupted. "You have
keep her on the track or she rambles. Mother, will you hur
up?"

Margaret's face, pink with indignation and effort, poppe
into view around the back of Christian's chair. He let out
yelp. "Watch what you're doing!"

"Oh, dear." Margaret disappeared from view. "Christia
you must believe I would never have let you come
Denmark if I had known Eric had contacted profession
criminals. It wasn't until that nasty little man dropped th
trunk on Marian that I realized the affair could be dangerou
There, darling, that's done it."

Christian brought his bleeding hands out from behind t
chair. Margaret crawled around and squatted at his feet.

"I'll do that." Christian snatched the knife and began sa
ing at the ropes around his ankles. "Why did you run away"

"Oh, that." Margaret glanced at Elizabeth and quick
glanced away. "We really must hurry, Christian. Whi
you're doing that I'll just . . ." She sidled toward the kn
rack.

"Oh, no, you don't," Christian shouted, so loudly th
Margaret jumped and Wolf's lip began to quiver. "Do
touch Elizabeth. I'll cut her loose. You just go on talking."

Margaret removed a knife from the rack and examine
regretfully. "Of course, dear, if you'd rather. But please
quick. Why did I run away? Why, because I thought El
abeth was one of the gang."

Christian paused in midslash; both he and Elizabeth turr
outraged stares on Margaret, who coughed and looked at
ceiling. "It was a logical deduction," she protested. "First
accident, then an unknown young woman turning up to
the vacated position. What was I to think? Her credenti

checked out, but that didn't prove anything; an impecunious, ambitious young person can be bribed. So I thought it better to—er—absent myself. I had to find Wolf, and I didn't dare try to get in touch with him while a member of the gang, as I believed, was watching every move I made."

She nodded benevolently as Christian finished cutting the ropes on his feet and went to perform the same service for Elizabeth. "Very nice, dear. You always were neat with your hands. Just like your father. "Where was I? Oh—my suspicions of Elizabeth. You will forgive me, won't you, dear girl? I'll try to make it up to you."

"I guess I can't blame you," Elizabeth admitted. Her hands were free. She twisted them together, trying to restore the circulation. "When did you realize I was harmless?"

"I wasn't absolutely certain until I reached this house," Margaret admitted. "Your supposed kidnapping could have been a trick, to win Christian's and my confidence. But when I heard what Schmidt and Radsky said about you I realized I had been mistaken. They wouldn't bother to put on an act for a senile old woman."

"Does Eric really have a cook?" Elizabeth asked.

"Yes, dear, of course. He sent Gertrud away after the others moved in. He was afraid for her safety. She is rather an outspoken person and she did not care for Mr. Schmidt and his friends, as she was quick to tell me when I called on her a few days ago. I fancied that by now Eric would be regretting his involvement, and would be very worried about Wolf. I felt sure he would play along with me. Which he did."

The bonds on Elizabeth's feet fell away, but she did not move. She looked incredulously at Margaret.

"You mean you just walked up to the house and asked for your—for Gertrud's—job back? You were taking an awful chance!"

"Not really. One old woman looks very much like another to persons without imagination or compassion. And," Margaret added complacently, "I am a master of disguise.

Are you through, dear? That's good. We really must be on
our way. I'll just free Eric."

Still clutching the carving knife, she trotted into the hall.

"Are you all right?" Christian asked, lifting Elizabeth into
his arms.

She clung to him, limp with relief and bewilderment. "I'm
numb. What do you suppose she has in mind now?"

"You ought to know better than to ask me."

"Christian, if she doesn't tell me what Margaret's bathrobe
is pretty soon, I am going to scream."

"Obviously it's a code word for some valuable."

"Obviously. But what?"

"We'll find out eventually," Christian said. His voice was
mild and incurious. Elizabeth looked at him anxiously. He
must be more seriously injured than she had realized.
Perhaps Schmidt's repeated blows had bruised his brain.

They moved apart as Margaret came back, followed by
Eric. She was spouting Danish at an alarming rate, waving
her arms to emphasize her point. The carving knife was still
in her hand; once or twice it narrowly missed Eric's nose,
but he was apparently used to her rhetorical style, for he only
ducked mechanically. Then Margaret shifted the knife to her
left hand, took a pencil from a pocket in her ragged skirt, and
scribbled on a piece of paper, which she handed to Eric. He
nodded. From a drawer in the cupboard he took a set of keys
and handed them to Margaret.

Elizabeth had no idea what they had said. Christian got
part of it. He didn't seem to like what he heard.

"Who did you tell him to call?" he demanded.

"Whom, dear. Even at a moment like this—"

"Don't stall, Margaret. You don't realize—"

"I do, Christian." They faced one another squarely. The
profiles might have been mirror images, but now Elizabeth
did not find the resemblance amusing. Margaret's face was
taut with strain, and when she continued, her voice shook
slightly. "Please trust me. Just this once—trust me."

"Okay."

"There isn't time to explain. . . . What?" Margaret's jaw dropped. "What did you say?"

"I said okay. What do we do now?"

"My dear!" Her lips parted, baring what appeared to be her entire supply of teeth. "We're going after them, of course. We'll take Eric's truck."

She was out the door before he could answer, running like a girl, her skirts raised to her knees.

The truck was an aged Ford pickup, battered and scarred by use. When they caught up with her, Margaret was trying to get into the driver's seat. Her short legs and long skirts made the process difficult.

"I'll drive," she said. "I know the way."

Christian's head jerked as if he had been slapped, but he made no objection, only assisted his mother into the truck with a brisk shove on the derriere. The engine sputtered into life as he got into the other seat and pulled Elizabeth onto his lap. He managed to close the door, although the truck was already moving backward at a good thirty miles an hour.

"The light switch is over there," he suggested, pointing.

"Oh. Yes, that is a good idea." Margaret changed gears noisily and sent the truck bucketing down the rutted lane.

Pressed against Christian, Elizabeth felt his body shaking uncontrollably. The dashboard lights illumined his tight-set lips and narrowed eyes, and she wondered if Margaret's driving, on top of the other perils of the night, had brought him to the brink of hysteria.

"I had better fill you in on some of it," Margaret said, peering nearsightedly through the dusty windshield. "Things are more desperate than I thought. I never dreamed Wolf would hide it so close to home."

"Where?" Elizabeth asked.

"In the barrow."

Christian emitted a brief bleating sound that Margaret interpreted as a question. Impatiently she went on, "Now, Christian, you know what a barrow is—one of the prehistoric mound tombs. I helped Fred Leinsdorf excavate it some years ago. That is how I met Eric and Wolf; the barrow is on their farm. It was a great disappointment—robbed in antiquity and in poor condition—so, although it is officially an Ancient Monument, no one has bothered with it since. Eric and Wolf have always considered it their private property. No doubt it is, in one sense; one of their own ancestors may have been buried there. Perhaps Wolf felt it was a suitable place. . . . But I am deeply concerned; the damp in that chamber is frightful and I pray no serious damage has ensued."

With no more warning than a sharp gasp she stamped on the brake. Christian's outflung arm saved Elizabeth from a cracked head as she was thrown toward the windshield. Then she saw what had prompted Margaret's stop. Square in the middle of the road, blinking in the headlights, sat a large long-eared rabbit.

Margaret put her head out the window. "Get out of the way, dear," she shouted. "That is a very dangerous place to sit."

The rabbit glanced disinterestedly in her direction and scratched one ear. Some perverse instinct told it the nature of the person it was dealing with, for it did not appear to be at all alarmed. After another, more urgent, request from Margaret, it got up and started hopping down the middle of the road. If it had run, Elizabeth would have thought it was frightened witless, but its pace was leisurely in the extreme and from time to time she saw its eyes glitter as it glanced casually over its shoulder.

"Exasperating animal," Margaret said, steering. Their progress was at the rate of approximately two miles an hour. "Christian, perhaps you had better get out and—"

"I'll do it," Elizabeth offered.

The rabbit seemed to be enjoying the game. It managed to keep just out of her reach for another hundred yards, its white tail flapping. Finally it got bored and disappeared into the brush on the side of the road.

Margaret did not pick up speed until they were some distance past the spot where the rabbit had vanished, but she made up for lost time thereafter. The other two were bounced around like popcorn in a popper. Crouched over the wheel and squinting, Margaret appeared to be enjoying herself, but when she spoke her voice was anxious.

"I fear we have lost too much time. I had calculated that they would run out of gas before they reached the hiding place. I did not know it was only a few miles away."

"You drained their gas tank?" Elizabeth asked. "Wasn't that dangerous? If they had noticed—"

"Eric did something to the gauge. I don't understand these things, I simply asked if it could be done and the clever man did it. They believe they have a full tank. However, the car is one of those European types that can go a good many miles on a small amount. Let me see. It has been a long time—but I think the turn is here!"

Elizabeth was flung from one side to the other as Margaret made a sweeping turn, without slackening speed. The truck ricocheted across the road and hit something with a loud crunch.

No one said anything for a while. In the dead silence Elizabeth heard the pensive chirping of a chorus of small animals or insects. The engine had stopped. From under the hood, which was tilted at a strange angle, came a thin plume of smoke. The headlights burned steadily.

❧ 13 ❧

"WE WOULD have had to leave the truck here anyway," Margaret said cheerfully. "If they are still at the barrow, the lights and the sound of the motor might alert them to our presence."

"If that crash didn't alert them, they must be at least ten miles away," Christian remarked.

Margaret pretended not to hear this. She drooped forward over the wheel. "Now that we are here, I am afraid to look. I fear the worst." The lights from the dash shadowed her features grotesquely. A few strands of plasticine or putty still clung to her chin like a scanty beard.

They got out of the truck. A stiff breeze was blowing, but Elizabeth was too excited to feel the cold. Clouds fled across the dark bowl of the sky, first baring and then concealing the lucent white globe of a moon nearing the full. The headlights made a wide path of yellow across a field broken by hedges and brambles; but the landscape to the left was illumined only by the fitful moonlight. Mysterious and indistinct, it might have been part of the Denmark of a thousand years in the past. There was no sign of life. Straight ahead and only a few hundred yards away, a dark shape loomed up against the star-sprinkled sky. Crowned with scrubby trees and ragged with bushes, it looked wholly natural until they were almost upon it. Then the strengthening moonlight silvered the angles of a block of stone, too sharply cut to be anything but the work of human hands. The rest of the stonework was hidden under brush.

"The entrance is around here, I think." Margaret looked uncertainly to her left. "I do wish I had a flashlight. Christian?"

"Such as it is." Christian took the small flash from his pocket and switched it on. The circle of light was limited, but it showed a depressing sight—tall grasses beaten down in an uneven but distinct path.

"Damn," Margaret said. "They've already been here. This way."

She plunged through the weeds, following a roughly circular route, with the mound on her right. Finally she stopped and turned to face the slope. The light showed trampled weeds and torn branches and, beyond them, a patch of exposed stonework, broken by a single gaping hole. Christian's little light was vanquished by the sullen darkness within. They saw only the green glistening of water-soaked lichen encrusting the walls of a narrow passage.

Margaret swore. "We sealed the passage when we closed the tomb ten years ago. Wolf would have had sense enough to replace the stones, but he probably didn't think of camouflaging the entrance. At any rate," she added, more cheerfully, "they had to sweat to pry those stones out. Mr. Schmidt wouldn't care for that."

"You're stalling again," Christian said. "Don't cop out now."

She sighed. "After you, dear."

Christian climbed over the pile of brush. He had to bend double to enter the passage, and his shoulders brushed the sides. After a moment his voice came back, weirdly amplified by echoes. "Come ahead. Nobody's here."

The passage was so low that even Margaret had to stoop to enter, but it was only eight or nine feet long. Christian put out a hand to guide them as they emerged from the passage and stood upright.

The chamber was some twelve feet in diameter and ten or twelve feet high in the center. The walls sloped sharply down from a domed top, like the interior of a beehive. The floor was of beaten earth, the walls of roughly shaped stone. Stone and earth glistened greasily in the light. Small pools of oily-looking water had collected in hollows. It was the gloomiest, most depressing place Elizabeth had ever seen, and the recent admission of air had not improved the musty scent of death and burial.

Christian turned the light toward the only object in the chamber—a low stone chest that rested against the far wall, blocking the entrance to what appeared to be another chamber beyond. The stone was neatly smoothed and polished, quite different from the rough construction of the tomb. Its soft-gleaming pallor had an undeniable beauty, and its function was evident from its dimensions—six feet long by three and a half wide by two feet high. It was a marble coffin, or sarcophagus; and it was open. The slab of marble that had sealed it lay to one side.

Slowly Margaret moved toward it. Christian followed with the light and shone it down into the sarcophagus. A moan of pure anguish came from Margaret.

"Too late," she murmured, like a Greek tragic chorus. "Too late, too late, too late."

The objects that covered the bottom of the coffin bore little resemblance to a decent burial—disarticulated bones, with strips of leathery flesh hanging from them, a tangled heap of fabric, like the contents of a rag bag. Delicately Margaret lifted one long fragment from the debris. The light reflected from tarnished cloth of gold, in a pattern of flowers and twining leaves.

"I'm sorry, Mother," Christian said.

"We did our best. But the tragedy of it..." Margaret sighed. "Some people would say it doesn't matter—that the human tragedies, death and disease and starvation, are more important. They are, of course they are; but the two values aren't mutually exclusive. Human agony and the irretrievable loss of knowledge are both wrong, both unnecessary. They can and should be stopped. It's happening all the time, all over the world—a continual process of theft and destruction. Often the thieves wantonly destroy objects they can't steal. The laws are totally inadequate, and our own government refuses to pass legislation, much less enforce it, that would prevent the importation of stolen art and antiquities. Collectors, even museums, encourage thieves by buying from them, no questions asked. Oh, it makes me so angry!"

She moved restlessly around the chamber, her hands exploring the rough walls.

"Then why don't we stop talking and go after them?" Christian said. "They still have to get out of the country with their loot."

"There's no hurry now," Margaret said drearily, continuing to fumble at the wall. "We may as well wait here; we haven't any means of transportation now that I . . . Aha, here they are. I thought we might have left some."

Elizabeth couldn't see what she was holding until she struck a match and lit the wick of the candle she had found. There was a sizable bundle of them; Margaret lit one after the other with profligate speed and stuck them onto ledges on the stone in puddles of their own grease.

"Queen Margaret's bathrobe," Elizabeth murmured. "Not so obscure at that. It really was her robe they were after."

"Not so much the robe as the gems that ornamented it. And her jewels—rings, bracelets, crown . . . *aieh!*" The shriek made Elizabeth jump. Margaret darted back to the coffin, now illumined by a dozen candles. She plunged her hands into the debris. After a moment she looked up, wild-eyed and furious. "Her head," she stuttered. "The skull isn't here. They have stolen Margaret's head!"

II

This final profanation infuriated Margaret beyond all reason. Elizabeth couldn't see that it mattered very much, and Christian shared her opinion.

"That's a minor catastrophe," he said.

"Carrying it around in a—in a gunny sack or brown paper bag!" Margaret wrung her hands. "Queen Margaret's head!"

Elizabeth decided some distraction was called for. "I don't understand how she got here. Her tomb is in Roskilde."

"Her tomb, but never her body." The prospect of lecturing restored Margaret's calm. "She was originally buried in the abbey church at Sorø, with her son and her husband. Bishop Lodehat decided to move her to Roskilde when the new cathedral was completed. They cared about such things then, you know. People still do, in fact, or they wouldn't move bodies back to their native earth.

"The monks at Sorø didn't want to give Margaret up, but they knew Lodehat would resort to force if he had to—oh, I know it sounds ludicrous, but have you forgotten how the Venetians stole the bones of Saint Lawrence from Cairo, hiding them in vats of pork fat, which was so abhorrent to the Muslim guards that they didn't bother to inspect the boxes? The abbot of Sorø also resorted to trickery. He hid Margaret's body and let the Bishop carry off an empty coffin, which was duly interred with all pomp and ceremony. For five and a half centuries the secret was kept and passed on from father to son as a sacred trust. Eric's ancestors must have been monks at the abbey, or perhaps skilled workmen who assisted in Margaret's secret burial."

"And Eric betrayed that trust," Christian said.

"He needed money." Margaret gave a soft, humorless laugh. "There's your classic conflict—human suffering versus ancient treasures. A small farmer has a hard time making a living these days, even in Denmark. And there was Wolf. They have no other family; Eric couldn't bear the idea that Wolf would be left to the tender mercies of the state after he died. He betrayed the ancient trust to help his brother. I cannot judge him."

There was a brief silence. Christian, obviously impressed and moved, stared thoughtfully at the floor.

"By this time," Margaret said, "Eric was the only one who remembered the old story. He broke into the abbey and, with Wolf's help, stole Margaret's coffin. Then he was faced with the problem of marketing his find. Schmidt and Radsky had the necessary contacts. They are members of an unusual and specialized profession—thieves of art and antiquities. How Eric got in touch with them I don't know, that is the one piece of information he refused to give me, so I suppose he has friends who acted as go-betweens—people to whom he feels loyalty.

"Wolf took an instant dislike to the members of the gang, especially Radsky. I'm sure other motives influenced him—remorse, religious scruples, superstitious fear of disturbing the dead. At any rate, before they could complete their arrangements to dispose of the treasure, Wolf stole the coffin, hid it here, and fled, after writing a frantic letter to me. The poor boy never thought of telephoning me; and I admit that the complexities of an overseas collect call would tax a stronger brain than his. It was two weeks before I could get here, and he was on the run the entire time, with Schmidt and Radsky close on his heels. His nerves were quite shattered and he was running from shadows—even mine!

"In the meantime one of the gang, looking for a clue among Wolf's things, found the rough drafts of the letter he had written me. With their criminal contacts it wasn't difficult for them to find out what flight I was taking and to prepare a scheme that would admit a spy into our midst. You see, they couldn't be sure Wolf had not already told me where he had hidden the coffin. When I refused to hire Schmidt, their next move was to incapacitate the hotel staff so that Cheryl would be hired as telephone operator. I didn't dare call or write you after that—"

"Aha," Christian said. "So you were in touch with Roger and Marie."

"They have their own private line," Margaret said. "I couldn't tell them the truth, it might have been dangerous for them, but they agreed to keep Cheryl on, though she was quite inadequate for the job. I feared that if she was let go the gang might try something more desperate. That was a slight error on my part, I admit. It led to the kidnapping of Elizabeth."

"That wasn't your only error," her son said critically. "Margaret, hasn't it occurred to you that Radsky and Schmidt couldn't have managed all this skulduggery by themselves? You keep talking vaguely about their criminal contacts, but—"

"Yes, darling, of course. I know just what you mean. Trust me."

"I've gone this far, I might as well go all the way," her son said resignedly. "Would you mind telling me why we are sitting in this dismal hole?"

"Waiting for help to arrive, of course." Margaret lowered herself gingerly onto the corner of the coffin. "I don't think she would mind," she murmured. "I told Eric to telephone. He is waiting for my call, but it will take a while for him to get here all the way from Copenhagen."

The shift in reference only confused Christian for a moment. "I hope," he said, very calmly, "that 'he' is not Grundtvig. Because if that's who you summoned to your rescue, we had better make tracks."

Margaret let out a crow of laughter, like an aging Peter Pan. "My dear, I have underestimated you—and though you may doubt it, my opinion of you has always been high. No, I did not summon Niels Grundtvig. I sincerely hope he is miles away from here."

"I cannot resist that," said a voice from the pitch-dark entrance to the barrow. "What a perfect cue for my entrance!"

They saw the gun first, clutched in a pudgy hand. The rest of Grundtvig followed.

For the first time in their erratic acquaintance Elizabeth saw Margaret genuinely taken aback. "How the devil did you get here?" she gasped.

Grundtvig gestured airily with his left hand. The right hand, holding the gun, remained steady.

"Radsky is a dependable man. He telephoned twice tonight—first when Wolf was taken prisoner, the second time after he had discovered the location of Margaret's bathrobe. I was well on my way by the time the second call came through; I have, of course, a telephone in my car. I decided to come by way of the barrow to make sure all was well. Seeing the abandoned truck, I feared trouble. And, you see, I was right."

He beamed at them like a genial grandfather. Elizabeth shook her head dizzily. She had begun to harbor doubts about Grundtvig herself, but she still found it difficult to believe.

"You suspected me, young Christian," Grundtvig said. "Where did I go wrong?"

For once the slighting adjective did not seem to bother Christian. "It was a lot of little things, none conclusive in itself. We overheard Radsky and Schmidt talking about some unnamed man in Copenhagen who was working with them. This man clearly was in a position to get information and gain access to certain places and do various things an ordinary criminal couldn't do. Then there was the severed finger. A highly placed police official would have access to a wide assortment of cadavers. Kidnapping Elizabeth was another of your mistakes. That was a subtle touch—too subtle to have occurred to a gang whose weapons were guns and blackjacks. The night we visited you at your place you realized that I—that I'd do anything to keep her safe, and that I would put pressure on Margaret to give in to your demands."

"Ah." Grundtvig looked relieved. "Not so bad; I am glad to hear it was no more than that. And you, Margaret? I con-

fess I was hurt that you did not come to me when you needed
help."

"I recognized you," Margaret said simply. "At Tivoli,
when I was riding the carousel. Roger had informed me
about the ransom note, and I was worried about Christian. I
know you too well, Niels. Did you think a false mustache
and unfamiliar clothes would deceive me?"

Grundtvig's blue eyes softened. There were old memories
in the glances they exchanged, and for a moment Elizabeth
saw Grundtvig as he must have looked fifteen, even ten years
earlier, before wrinkles and fat had turned him into a jolly
Father Christmas.

"Now you must not say that sort of thing," Grundtvig said
pettishly. "It is not fair. A professional must not be distracted
from his duty by sentiment."

"But how could you?" Margaret exclaimed. "You, of all
people."

"You know why—you, of all people!" Grundtvig turned
the gun, and a hostile scowl, on Christian. "He does it to you
as my daughter does to me—'Mama, don't do this,' and
'Papa, don't do that.' 'Sit down and rest your old bones,
mama'; 'Eat your gruel, Papa, and die!' Once the old were
honored and respected. Now they throw us in the garbage.
They want me to retire, can you believe it? Now, when I am
at the peak of my powers—to sit hour after hour in that drab
little house and amuse myself by whittling Viking ships and
tending my garden. I hate gardening!"

A chorus of ghostly echoes flung back a passionate
accord. Margaret winced. "Oh, Niels . . ."

"Don't *you* patronize me, Margaret."

"I'm sorry, Niels."

"I am sorry too. Why did you have to interfere? You have
narrowed my choices down to two. You or me, Margaret.
The survival of one of us means the destruction of the other."

Try as she would, Margaret could not keep her eyes from
shifting sideways toward her son; but she knew the futility of

that kind of appeal. It was Christian who said, "You can't kill all three of us before I get you, Grundtvig."

"Oh, can't I? There speaks the despicable arrogance of youth. God, I hate that! You are stupid as well as arrogant, boy. I will back into this passageway and pick you off one by one."

"Well, I'm not just going to stand here and let you—"

"For goodness' sake, Christian, you're just making him angry," his mother said in exasperation. "Don't move." For she, as well as Elizabeth, had observed the tensing of Christian's muscles. "He isn't going to shoot us."

"You think not?" Grundtvig tried to look menacing, but his lips would shape no more sinister expression than a pout.

"I know. You've spent forty years fighting beastliness and savagery, Niels. You have bent the law a little lately, but killing us would shatter the foundations of your soul. And if you ever did kill anybody," Margaret concluded, "it would-n't be me."

In the silence a drop of water splashed into a puddle with a sound like thunder. Elizabeth's eyes were riveted on Grundtvig's hand. The universe had shrunk to a single point—a shining weapon and the plump white fingers that held it. Grundtvig's arm tensed. He flung the gun angrily against the wall.

"Curse you, Margaret, why are you always right?"

"At least I'm *old* and right," she said, her voice rough with what might have been relief, or laughter, or perhaps tears. "Niels, my dear . . ."

She rose from her incongruous seat and held out her hand. Grundtvig took it in his. "I couldn't hurt you, Margaret."

"I know, my dear."

"Then it's a good thing I arrived when I did," said Schmidt, emerging from the tunnel.

"Oh, for God's sake!" Christian, who had relaxed with a pent-up burst of breath, spoke more in anger than in sorrow. "How many more people are out there?"

"Just me," Schmidt said modestly, resting his gun hand on his lifted arm. "Radsky and Cheryl are trying to siphon gas out of the truck. That was a smart idea, leaving us with an almost empty tank. It would have worked, too, if some damned fool hadn't wrecked the truck and left the lights shining like a beacon."

A stronger, nobler man than Christian Rosenberg could not have refrained from shooting a critical glance at his mother. Margaret looked stricken. Grundtvig put a protective arm around her.

"There is no need for killing, Schmidt. Leave them here unharmed, and I will accompany you. With my influence you can be quickly out of Denmark."

"No deal, Grandpa."

"Grandpa?" Grundtvig lunged forward, apoplectic with rage. Schmidt indicated the gun. Grundtvig came to a stop, breathing hard.

"Can't trust you now," Schmidt went on. "Too bad. With your connections we could have emptied all the museums in Europe. But we'll get by."

Christian took a step to one side, away from the others.

"Where do you think you're going?" Schmidt demanded.

"Broadening your target area." Christian continued to sidle sideways.

"You want it first, I guess," Schmidt said, taking aim.

Christian told him what he could do with the gun. "Why, Christian," Margaret exclaimed in shocked tones. "Shame on you."

Schmidt turned toward her. Christian took another step. Schmidt turned toward him. "Don't shoot," Margaret shrieked. Schmidt turned toward her.

"I think that should do it," Christian said.

"Right," Margaret replied, as the weapon wavered between them. Simultaneously she and Christian threw themselves to the floor.

The gun went off. Bullets bounced madly around the domed roof. Schmidt's foot slipped on the greasy floor, and

Christian, whose dive downward had taken him close to his goal, put out a long arm and grabbed Schmidt's ankle. Schmidt toppled backward. His head hit the curved ceiling with a ripe crunch. The gun went flying off into space.

The Rosenbergs rose to their respective feet and eyed one another over Schmidt's unconscious figure with identical grins of self-congratulation.

"Very nice," Margaret said breathlessly. "Now, then, we seem to have two guns. You take one and I—"

Christian stopped her with a bone-cracking hug, lifting her clean off her feet. "You are the slickest, trickiest schemer I ever met," he told her. "But I'll be damned if I am going to turn you loose on an unsuspecting world with a gun in your hand. Relax and let the hired help clean up the mess." He set her down. "Come on, Grundtvig, we'll cut 'em off at the pass!"

"Well!" Margaret said, when the men had departed, dragging Schmidt's body with them. "How that boy has changed! Shall we go, Elizabeth?

"Please, Margaret. Let him handle this."

"I couldn't agree more, my dear. But there is no reason why we have to wait here. Such a dank, damp, dismal place. Most unhealthy."

Hoisting up her skirts, she bent over and entered the passageway. Elizabeth followed closely, ready to wrestle Margaret to the ground if the latter's pugnacious instinct overcame her common sense.

The clouds had blown away. The sky was a dazzle of stars, with a serene silver moon as a centerpiece. Elizabeth breathed deeply of the sweet night air. What a wonderful mechanism was the human lung! She rendered sincere thanks that hers were still operating.

Her suspicions of Margaret had been unfounded. The older woman sat down on a convenient stone and motioned Elizabeth to join her. From that vantage point they could see the glimmering path of the truck's headlights. They had barely seated themselves when a shot broke the peace of the night. Elizabeth started to her feet.

"It's quite all right," Margaret said. "That, I believe, was a warning shot. A fusillade would have followed had the criminals determined to resist. Niels is quite good at this sort of thing, you know. And Mr. Radsky is not the man to risk his neck for a hopeless cause."

Elizabeth returned to her seat. Margaret threw a warm, plump art around her.

"My dear Elizabeth! How can I thank you? The change you have wrought in Christian is little short of miraculous. I always knew he had it in him, but—"

"You did?" Elizabeth was just beginning to realize how tired she was. Her reactions, mental and physical alike, were slowed by fatigue.

"Of course. He's just like his father, my dear. Theodore was a prim, proper young aristocrat in his early days; it took the war to bring out his better side. I tried to encourage Christian, but I ought to have known it was not a mother's influence he needed."

The dark horizon blossomed with bright stars that soon resolved themselves into automobile headlights. A full-scale procession seemed to be approaching. The lights converged and stopped near the truck.

"That must be Frederick," Margaret said. "No doubt he made the best possible time, but I must say that if we had depended on him, we would be in a pretty pickle."

"Are you talking about Dr. Leinsdorf?"

"He was my back-up man," Margaret said complacently. "I got in touch with him before I went to the farm. He is quite abnormally imaginative for a Ph.D.; he knew of the vandalism at Sorø, of course, and when Christian told him what *he* knew, clever Frederick put two and two together. I had to insist that he refrain from interfering until I had succeeded in freeing you and Christian. His was, of course, the telephone number I gave Eric."

A murmur of conversation floated up to them from the group gathered around the truck.

"They seem to be having quite a nice time," Margaret said. "Let's just let them congratulate one another, shall we? Men have such frail little egos, poor dears; it would be cruel of us to deflate them."

Her warm, motherly embrace felt marvelous. Elizabeth leaned against her shoulder. Margaret patted her. "Poor child, you must be exhausted. You've done awfully well, you know. And after all my unfair, cruel suspicions. I'll make it up to you, dear. Trust me."

🎀 14 🎀

"THE GUNS of Kronberg Castle still menace the narrow strait between Denmark and Sweden, just as they did four hundred years ago, when Frederic the Second built the fortress to extract tolls from ships entering the Baltic. Modern visitors pay homage, not to the spirit of the mercantile monarch, but to a more antique and possibly apocryphal ghost. Kronberg is also known as the castle of Elsinore. The only Hamlet who has ever prowled the dim corridors is a modern actor; Kronberg was not finished until centuries after the death of the Viking prince Amleth, on whose adventures Shakespeare is reputed to have based his play."

"I know all that," Elizabeth said irritably, as Christian paused in his reading from the guidebook. "Just shut up for five minutes and let me absorb the atmosphere."

They were standing near the spot where the ghost of Hamlet's father had *not* appeared—despite the claims of some of the guides who now haunt the castle. Margaret was a tactful twenty feet away, pretending not to watch them. Her costume had been carefully designed as a tribute to the spirit of Hamlet. It consisted of tight black slacks (not even Margaret had the effrontery to appear in hose) and a black tunic over a white blouse whose sleeves were so full they hung down over her hands when the air was still, and bil lowed like sails when the breezes blew. Her hair was now blond. Atop her head was a black velvet beret to which she had fixed, somewhat insecurely, a long feather. The profile contemplating the battlements reminded Elizabeth of a photo she had once seen, of John Gielgud in the role; but even Gielgud's nose was not the equal of Margaret's.

Christian closed his guidebook and glanced at his mother. "I still don't see how she got away with it," he muttered.

Elizabeth knew what he was referring to. They had discussed the subject a number of times, but Christian remained incredulous.

"Nobody wanted a scandal, including the police," she said. "One of their best men, cracking up after years of faithful service ... And with Margaret lying like a trooper, contradicting everything Schmidt and Radsky said—it was her word and Grundtvig's against a pair of known criminals."

"She's told so many lies it's a wonder God hasn't struck her dumb," her son remarked admiringly. "The way she got Wolf and Eric off—"

"Same principle," Elizabeth interrupted. She was getting bored with the subject. "Schmidt's and Radsky's word against Margaret's and Grundtvig's. Wolf may even get a reward for saving a national treasure. And Leinsdorf will get the gems for the museum, so he's happy. They should be quite a tourist attraction."

Christian hunched his shoulders, as if a cool breeze had struck through his jacket. "I'll never forget the sight of Margaret cradling that awful mummified head. I thought for a minute she was going to talk to it. 'Now, dear, everything is just fine, and we'll soon get you back into your nice coffin.' Brrr!"

"It was nasty looking," Elizabeth admitted. "I wish I hadn't seen it; I'd rather think of the queen as Margaret conjured her up that night at Tivoli—young and lovely and courageous. But, Christian ... Did you happen to notice—well—a certain resemblance?"

"Especially around the nose," Christian agreed. The corners of his mouth turned up in a grin. He put his arm around Elizabeth. "Brace yourself, darling, she's reading her guidebook again."

Elizabeth sagged against him. "I can't take much more," she moaned. "I wish I'd never mentioned sightseeing. Christian, she's going through the book page by page, checking things off."

"She's trying to be nice."

"I know. That's what makes it so awful."

"I thought you wanted to see the sights. There wouldn't be anything else you would prefer doing, would there?"

"Since you ask, we haven't had five minutes alone!"

"That's all I wanted to know. You helpless women always need a man to get you out of trouble. Get ready to be rescued again."

Margaret trotted toward them. The feather in her hat jerked awkwardly up and down with each step. She pushed several yards of billowing white sleeve out of the way and pointed to her wristwatch.

"We must hurry, darlings, if we are to reach Fredensborg Slot. Since Her Majesty was kind enough to give us permission to see the royal apartments, I do not think it would be courteous to be late."

"We certainly mustn't keep the queen waiting," Christian said. "But that's it, Margaret. No more sightseeing. In fact, I want you to leave. Go home. Tomorrow, if possible."

"Go home?" Margaret's eyes widened. "You want me to—"

Christian tried to take her hands, but was foiled by flowing white silk. "You're only doing this as a favor to Elizabeth. You've seen every sight in Denmark a dozen times, and you're dying to get back to your book. We don't need a chaperone, Mother. We're both over the age of consent."

Margaret was silent for a moment. Then she said, "Are you proposing to turn me loose on an unsuspecting world, unsupervised and uncontrolled?"

"It's high time I did, isn't it?" Christian said gravely.

Margaret stood on tiptoe and flung both arms around Christian's neck, smothering him in yards of silk. He clawed at the folds and freed his mouth.

"Fredensborg Slot, remember? We don't want to be late."

Elizabeth discreetly fell behind as the Rosenbergs, moving as one, walked toward the exit. They did not link arms, or even look at one another, but they obviously enjoyed complete accord and understanding. After a while Christian said, "One stipulation—"

"Yes, dear, I will. You can count on it."

"Will what?"

"Let you in on any new and interesting . . . I think 'caper' is an appropriate word in this context."

Smiling, Christian turned his head and looked down at her. The feather swept across his face. He sneezed violently.

Elizabeth watched them affectionately, but there was a degree of apprehension in her mind. Once she had thought that being Margaret's daughter-in-law might prove to be a less than peaceful occupation. With both Rosenbergs on the warpath, flexing their muscles and looking for excitement. . . .

An invisible tendril of anxiety must have tickled Margaret's mind-reading equipment. She glanced over her shoulder, all thirty-two teeth on display.

"Don't worry, darling. Everything is going to be wonderful. Trust me!"

By the year 2000, 2 out of 3 Americans could be illiterate.

It's true.

Today, 75 million adults... about one American in three, can't read adequately. And by the year 2000, U.S. News & World Report envisions an America with a literacy rate of only 30%.

Before that America comes to be, you can stop it... by joining the fight against illiteracy today.

Call the Coalition for Literacy at toll-free **1-800-228-8813** and volunteer.

Volunteer Against Illiteracy. The only degree you need is a degree of caring.

Ad Council Coalition for Literacy